ETHICAL PRINCIPLES IN
THEORY AND PRACTICE

ETHICAL PRINCIPLES

IN THEORY AND PRACTICE

AN ESSAY IN MORAL PHILOSOPHY

By HANS DRIESCH, PH.D.

Hon. LL.D. Aberdeen;
Hon. M.D. Hamburg; Hon. Sc.D. Nanking;
Foreign Member of the Linnean Society and of the Academy
of Science, Heidelberg; Member of Phi Kappa Phi; late President
of the Society for Psychical Research, London, and of the
Society for Psychical Research, Athens; Professor of
Philosophy in the University of Leipzig

Translated by
W. H. JOHNSTON, B.A.

LONDON
GEORGE ALLEN & UNWIN LTD
MUSEUM STREET

*The German original, "Die Sittliche Tat," first published in
Leipzig, in 1927*
FIRST PUBLISHED IN GREAT BRITAIN IN 1930

PREFACE

WHEN a man has reached the age of sixty years he has some justification for writing on Ethics; for at that age he has himself experienced many of those human situations which form the subject of Ethics, and is therefore acquainted with them in that detail which is essential for a complete ethical system. At that age he is also more firmly convinced than ever that Ethics, as soon as it passes beyond questions of mere meaning—which is its proper task, although too often it is neglected—must be a confession and no more. The reader may reply that he is not interested in confessions. History, however, shows us two great examples which may yet cause him to retract. For at least they can stimulate the reader to thought, and perhaps to contradiction. That, too, would suffice, if only there is thought.

Almost all the existing modern systems of Ethics deal with formal definitions, and at bottom repeat more or less the same thing about them in slightly different words. In this work these are a side-issue, and therefore are treated briefly. Their treatment in Section I is based upon my theoretical works, the *Theory of Order* and the *Theory of Reality*, but will be intelligible to those who are not acquainted with those works. Our chief concern is moral teaching—that is, the practical element. For this very reason questions of the day, especially political questions, play a great part in this work, although of course they do not do so in a form specifically adapted to definite persons, countries, or events, though such may have been present to the mind of the author. After all, the question of peace is a political question, and this question is *the* ethical question *par excellence*; so that it is not too much to say that in our time this question and all that is connected with it takes precedence over all others.

This book does not constitute a political dogma or a political science in the proper sense. Least of all is it written in a party spirit. No one party will be entirely in agreement with it; but the author hopes that statesmen may profit by it. For a true statesman, especially if he governs, must act in accordance with ethical rules, even though he knows that in practice he will fall far short of perfect compliance, since he is operating upon men, and is in conflict with their stupidity, ignorance, and sloth, and sometimes with their ill will. In such a case even the best statesman knows that, of the good at which he aims, only a very small portion is attainable. His office is full of renunciation, nor can it be otherwise. However, the smallest practical progress towards the good is none the less valuable.

The man who preaches a code has an easier task than he who has to realize one; for paper is long-suffering. Hence we may freely admit that progress towards the good, however small, actually realized by the statesman is of greater moral value than an ethical system, however perfect, set up by a philosopher. The highest value of all is to be assigned to a life lived as a pattern in Ethics.

There is a mean position between the ethical philosopher (the preacher of a code) and the statesman (the man who realizes a code) which is occupied by the teacher in the wide sense of the word, which also comprehends the priest, and even good publicists. We may describe the teacher as the man who spreads the code. It is to the teacher that our book makes a special appeal; for in him resides the greatest power to convey ethical truth, and consequently he does the preparatory work for the man who realizes it. We hope to convince many teachers of the truth of what we teach; for we demand most rigorously that they shall teach nothing but that of which they really are convinced.

We have already established a contrast between the theoretical student of Ethics and the statesman, and we said that the office of the latter is more difficult, more full of renunciations, but also more important for the course of the world. There is another distinction connected with this. The student of Ethics is a philosopher, and as such he must make his postulates with absolute rigour. If they are hazy he will achieve nothing at all. If his postulates are exact—exceedingly exact—he may achieve a little, at least if they are perfectly just, for otherwise they may easily lead to the opposite of the end which is aimed at. The statesman on the other hand must exercise moderation even in his desires, which he must confine to that which is practically possible at any given time. He reaches nothing if he wants too much, although he may long to have the right to want everything. Hence the statesman is always involved in excuses, which in this work too will play a part equally necessary and regrettable. He *must* even make excuses where the student of Ethics *may* not excuse. It is here that renunciation lies for any statesman who has lofty ethical principles —that is, who keeps his eyes fixed on ethical rules in their most rigorous exactness. It is our hope that the world may have many such statesmen as we have described them.

In an external sense it is an accident that this book was begun in China and concluded in America: in an inner sense it is perhaps no accident.

HANS DRIESCH

LEIPZIG,
October 1927

CONTENTS

PAGE

PREFACE 7

PROLEGOMENA 15

I

1. THEORETICAL ETHICS AND DOCTRINE OF MORALS 15
2. THE MEANING OF "IT OUGHT TO BE" 18
3. ETHICS AND FREEDOM 23
4. ETHICAL INTUITION, ETHICAL CAPACITY, AND GOOD WILL 25
5. ETHICAL JOY 29
6. DUTY AND FELLOWSHIP IN LIFE 34
7. THE PROBLEM OF APPLIED ETHICS 37
   A. Its Metaphysical Foundation 37
   B. Are there particular Moral Feelings? 40
   C. The Danger of Feelings due to Habit 47
8. THAT WHICH OUGHT TO BE AND THAT WHICH IS 48
9. CONSPECTUS OF THE FUNDAMENTAL CONCEPTS OF ETHICS, WITH A TERMINOLOGY BASED UPON "VALUE" 50
10. THE PROBLEM OF CONCRETE ETHICS FURTHER CONSIDERED 59
11. THE ETHICAL AXIOM 64
12. THE ETHICAL PROBLEM RESTRICTED TO THE REAL 67

II

THE DOCTRINE OF DUTIES 70
1. WE HAVE NO DUTIES TOWARDS THE NON-LIVING 70
2. DUTIES TOWARDS "MY" PERSON 71
   A. Duties towards my Body 72
      a. My Body as bare living Entity. The First Point of Dichotomy 73
      b. My Body as an Instrument of the Soul 76
   B. Duties towards my Soul 78
      a. My Soul as Acting Entity in general 79
      b. My Soul as containing Particular Dispositions 81
      c. The Purity of my Soul 83

PAGE

3. DUTIES TOWARDS MY NEIGHBOUR, *qua* INDIVIDUAL PERSON   84

   A. Propagation. The First Apology   85

   B. General Remarks relating to that which is to follow:
       Egoism and Altruism   90

   C. The Commandment which forbids Killing   97

   D. Where Killing is prohibited generally, What Apologies
       can be brought forward?   101

   E. The Injunctions against inflicting Harm   103

   F. The Rule which enjoins the Fostering of Talents   106

   G. The Injunction to tell the Truth   109

   H. Property: When is it justified?   112

4. DUTIES TOWARDS GROUPS   117

   A. Marriage   118

   B. Birth-Control   120

   C. The Nations   123

   D. The State   124

     a. The Internal Functions of the State   126

       α. General Remarks   126

       β. Penal Codes   128

       γ. Social Questions   129

       δ. Education. Schools   130

     b. The Constitution   136

     c. The State and its Relation to other States   143

       α. War   144

       β. War-Guilt   155

       γ. Conscription, Police, etc.   159

       δ. Patriotism and its Manifestations   164

     d. Work within the State   171

       α. General Considerations   171

       β. Cosmopolitanism and Particularism. The League
          of Nations   172

       γ. The Nature of Peoples. Can They understand
          One Another?   176

       δ. Conclusion   186

CONTENTS

III

		PAGE
	ENLIGHTENMENT	191
1.	FALSE ENLIGHTENMENT AND GENUINE ENLIGHTENMENT	192
2.	GENUINE ENLIGHTENMENT	195
3.	RATIONALISM	200
4.	"REALPOLITIK"	203
5.	THE EFFECTS OF RATIONAL ENLIGHTENMENT	205
6.	OBSTACLES AND HOW THEY ARE OVERCOME	210

IV

	RELIGION AS THE AIM OF ENLIGHTENMENT	218
1.	THE RELIGIOUS STATE, RELIGION AND METAPHYSICS	218
2.	RATIONAL EMOTIONS	223
3.	TRUE ENLIGHTENMENT AND RELIGION	230
4.	RELIGIOUS DENOMINATIONS AND THE CHURCH	235
5.	DUALISM AND HOW IT IS OVERCOME	240
	INDEX	247

ETHICAL PRINCIPLES IN THEORY AND PRACTICE

I

PROLEGOMENA

I

THEORETICAL ETHICS & DOCTRINE OF MORALS

THERE is a doctrine which deals with the meaning of the word "moral" or "good", and with the manner in which these meanings are consciously apprehended; and this doctrine is wholly different from that which deals with the particular content of the good. I may know the meaning of "good", and I may realize the form in which this meaning becomes an object of my thought; but it does not follow from this that I know which individual event in a particular instance is good. To speak in a perfectly general way, I may know that a certain event ought to take place in conformity with the principle of the fundamental nature of Order; but this knowledge does not decide in the least as to what "ought" to happen here and now.

This fact is known to all, although all are not perhaps perfectly acquainted with its ultimate reasons.

Besides this we all know that the general doctrine of the meaning of "good in general" and our acquaintance with particular good furnishes the material for a system of rules for men of good will.

Thus we recognize the inner multiplicity of so-called Ethics at the very beginning.

We can also explain our meaning by applying certain well-known terms from the philosophy of Kant.

The doctrine of the meaning of the terms "moral", "good", "it ought to be", like the doctrine which deals with the manner of their apprehension, belongs wholly to theoretical philosophy, and more particularly, in the general sense of the term, to logic, or, where we are concerned with the manner of apprehension, to preliminary logic. Indeed, Kant's great work in moral philosophy, in spite of its name, in the main confines itself to this theme. The doctrine also which considers what acts in particular, if they were to take place, would deserve the name of good is in the first instance a matter of intuition, or, literally, of theory.

But it is possible for the universal as well as the particular doctrine to become a set of rules which apply immediately to $\pi\rho\acute{a}\tau\tau\epsilon\iota\nu$, to action, for those who are of good will. This alone is "practical philosophy".

It is true that here we must not forget that the judgment "it ought (or ought not) to be" can be made with reference to every event which affects living subjects in any manner, and more particularly men. Misfortunes, too, are classed under the category "it ought not to be", which implies a tacit accusation against an unknown x. In the narrower sense of the term alone Ethics is a theoretical science, and as such is a doctrine of human actions; and of course it is in this sense alone that it can be the basis of rules.

In the following pages we speak of this human science of Ethics.

Human Ethics in general thus has two parts, a theoretic and a practical, and each of these is subdivided into two parts, one of which has for subject the good in general, and the other, the concrete good.

At this place the phenomenon of *good will* must be discussed: this constitutes a separate and intermediate section.

"If I am *homo bonae voluntatis*, what must be my line of action in every case which is made possible by the state of my inner and my outer world?" The main task of the doctrine of practical Morals is to find an answer to this question. But such an answer can have no other foundation than the answer to our theoretical questions, and more particularly to the second: "What exactly must be the nature of actions in order that they shall deserve the predicate of *good*, it being supposed that the meaning of this term is clear?"

It might be said of Ethics that, in so far as it is a theory, it may be compared to the doctrines which deal with the phenomenological nature of the axioms of geometry, with their content and with the particular conclusions, the individual theorems, which follow from these. In that case practical Ethics might be compared with applied geometry. At the crucial point, however, the comparison fails; for in geometry the doctrine of the content of the axioms and of the conclusions which follow thence has the same definitive or "apodeictic" character as belongs to the doctrine of the phenomenological nature of the axioms—that is, to the recognition of the fact that they *are* axioms. In Ethics, on the other hand, it is possible to apprehend the phenomenological and denotational nature of "good in general"; but everything that relates to the content of these terms falls short of these apprehensions in certainty, as much as in physics everything that is empirical falls short in certainty of the doctrine of the universal natural categories, and that in a much higher degree. Hence results the same lack of certainty in the doctrine of practical morals. In any event, the latter remains a practical application based upon theory.

2

THE MEANING OF "IT OUGHT TO BE"

The meaning of the expression "it ought to be" has been elaborated in greater detail in my *Doctrine of Order*, and has been further explained in my *Doctrine of Reality*, and this also applies to the somewhat narrower word "good", which in contrast to the universal "it ought to be" is restricted to human action. These discussions related both to the ontological value and to the manner of apprehension of these two expressions, as well as to their objects.

Ontologically "it ought to be" and "good" are particular and definitive order-denotations which are apprehended in certain empirical facts as the forms which saturate these facts. These empirical facts are of a psychological nature when the contents of my will, or of my soul, are called "good" or "bad"; on the other hand, they are physical (at least immediately) when they are used to describe my own actions or those of others, although in such a case the indirect transition is always made from the action as motion-event to the soul-element (my own or that of an other) which is supposed to be its foundation. In this process the meaning is taken for granted of such words as "soul" and "belonging to the soul" and of such concepts as "the other ego", "the psychic-corporeal person", and so forth. It must be remarked here that our system of Ethics does not imply the acceptance of my own system of logical concepts. The contents of this book are intelligible to those who approach them from the point of view of a wholly different logical system, or even from the point of view of the set of concepts which prevail in everyday life.

I intuit the meaning of "good" in the same manner in which I intuit the meaning of "straight", or in the same manner in which I know the proposition of the one and only possible straight line: this knowledge has a peculiar finality. And here it is possible to make a further comparison with respect to geometry. In the first instance I know the meaning of "parallel" as a meaning which exists in a clear and definitive manner; I know it intuitively, although I do not intuit optically. In the second instance I apprehend by means of reflection that the space in which this term has a significance is a simplest possible case, not among "possible spaces", as the metageometricians would have it, but among systems of spatial relations. The case is similar with Ethics. In the first instance I have knowledge of the meaning of "good" as a meaning which exists in a clear and definite manner; and in the second instance I am then able to analyse this meaning, so to speak—a state of affairs which unfortunately does not appear to hold good for ethical propositions whose content applies to particulars.

Or does it, after all, hold good? This precisely is what we shall investigate in this book.

At an earlier period[1] I had analysed the "instinctive" meaning of "good"—that is, quite literally, the meaning of "good" which is kindled within me—and I had come to the conclusion that all that is called "good" relates somehow to some supra-personal totality which is in process of becoming, a totality whose becoming is regarded as a true development towards a teleological Whole or "end", it being assumed that I would say of this Whole, were it known to me, "this ought to be". The teleological Whole ought to be, and it possesses completely the character of finality—I intentionally avoid the word *value* because of its ambiguity—and therefore this or that action which tends towards the realization of the teleo-

---

[1] *Ordnungslehre*, Second edition, 1923, pp. 423 *sqq.*; *Wirklichkeitslehre*, Second edition, 1922, p. 177.

logical Whole *ought* to be, and for this reason it is called "good".

In the course of years I have come to view more sceptically the doctrine that so-called history, which is our subject here, is a true evolution. I shall express this scepticism in the new edition of my *Doctrine of Reality*. At present I think that another view, which had also been considered at an earlier time, is more probable—the view which holds that everything that belongs to the history of man is merely of a cumulatively psychological nature. I think that men have always been essentially the same, so long at least as phylogenetically they were men. In that case humanity in general, as I have said previously, is probably no more than a stage in a course of evolution which remains wholly metaphysical and manifests itself to me in a merely phenomenal manner in the earthly phase, which is one among many, the term *evolution* being taken in its full and strict sense.

If this is the truth, then "it ought to be" must not, of course, be referred to the final whole of a supra-personal historical evolution proper, since by assumption there is no such evolution: it would refer to the promotion of man in general and the community of man—where the latter would still be a totality—towards a state which earthly man cannot understand and which is that which ought to be and to which all earthly actions and all earthly states, even those which are socially the most perfect, are related merely as means.

There still remains, then, the relation to a future state,

which is to be attained in the course of world-history, which is apprehended only abstractly, but is approved. It seems to me that this formula is akin to the theoretical result which lies at the bottom of Kant's *Categorical Imperative*. However that may be, all our considerations to this point are part of the most general kind of logic, of "theoretic" philosophy. But now that we have reached the end of these most general considerations we may effect the transition, however indefinite, to the practical application, or to the doctrine of ethics.

"If you wish to be able to call your actions good, you must act in a certain manner." This is always the general form of the transition. Here Kant, of course, puts in place of "in a certain manner" the concept of a desired and universal law. My own injunction is equally indefinite and universal: "Act in such a way that you can believe that your action is promoting a future state of mankind accepted by you and approved in its nature, which state is *perhaps* the goal of a supra-personal evolution."

Here we have two injunctions: both accordingly belong to the doctrine of Ethics. But both are based on theoretic intuition, namely, on the propositions: "Such actions ought to be (or, are good), as are based upon maxims which (according to Kant) are desired by their subject as a universal law, or (according to me) aim at an approved future state of man."

If I wish to be able to call my actions good, these injunctions constitute a kind of imperative[1] for me. Thus

---

[1] But not more than a *kind* of imperative, for the Kantian Reason which gives itself its own laws is an impossibility is taken literally,

the imperative is not absolutely categorical, although it is so for the "good" man, which is meant to mean for the man part of whose nature it is that he wishes to be able to call his actions good.

Both these imperatives are very empty. Can we give them a content? This question once more brings us face to face with the particular task of this book.

3
ETHICS AND FREEDOM

At this point it becomes necessary to mention the problem of freedom, but, strange as it may sound, to do no more than mention it. For Ethics is a theoretical and dogmatic structure, and as such is not affected by the sense in which the problem of freedom is answered; and this, as will appear, is in the main true also of practical moral doctrine.

By "freedom" I mean here that the admission of a will-content, or its realization, is not determined: I mean the *liberum arbitrium indifferentiae*, and not that which Spinoza, and probably Kant, mean by "freedom". Details about the whole of the problem will be found at another place.[1]

For Ethics remain "Ethics"—that is a structure of particular concepts and propositions, valid in the field

as has been pointed out by many writers on Ethics. What Kant probably meant was, "I intuit as ethically definitive". At any rate, this is all that he ought to have meant.

[1] Driesch, *Metaphysik*, 1924, pp. 40–69, and Driesch, *Grundprobleme der Psychologie*, 1926, pp. 196 *sqq.*

of the "it ought to be" and indifferent to the existence or non-existence of freedom.

If freedom does not exist, two cases are possible. Either each ego is a member of a true supra-personal development; his ethical consciousness is an "epiphenomenon" whose function it is to indicate to him the part which it is his destiny to play in this evolution. Or else there is no such true evolution, and in that case the totality of all psychological events is mere cumulation— that is, there are in the personal ego details which point to a supra-personal totality, but there is no supra-personal evolution. In this case ethical consciousness is likewise an "epiphenomenon", which indicates to the individual in an abstract form his ultimate goal—a goal which the totality of all individuals is destined to reach by means of a very slow cumulative process. In that case the individual, if a metaphor may be borrowed from mechanics, realizes only the state of dynamic equilibrium which will be reached some day, as well as the degree by which the present state falls short of it.

If, on the other hand, there is freedom in the true sense of indeterminism, then the state of affairs is, of course, totally different in *one* respect. In that case every piece of conscious knowledge, including the intuition of ethical meanings, provides material for the ego, and it is the part of the ego freely to determine whether this material is or is not to be realized.

It thus appears that intuition as such, and the whole of the theoretical and doctrinal system of meanings which is based upon it, remain unchanged in each case. There is a difference at one point only, namely, at the transition from theory to practice—that is, to ethical doctrine as a system of injunctions, where we pass from *it ought to be* to *thou shalt*, or rather to *I ought*.

For if there is no such thing as freedom, then this *I ought* has the significance only of an "as if". I have the illusion that "I ought", but in fact I can do only that which I am determined to do. If there is freedom, then *I ought* in truth, and I can in the sense of "yes" or "no". But in both cases I experience that *I ought* immediately as conscience, and so long as I am still naïve I have no idea of the problem of freedom and of its difficulties. Accordingly moral doctrine, too, can be formulated as a system of injunctions alternatively with or without freedom; only in the latter case it is an illusion for those who scrutinize ultimate causes. Thus we have some justification for saying that if freedom is rejected moral doctrine proper becomes a matter of slight importance. But the theory remains absolutely unchanged, with or without freedom.

We shall revert, then, to the problem of freedom: but we shall do so only at the end of this work.

4

ETHICAL INTUITION, ETHICAL CAPACITY, AND "GOOD WILL"

We now revert to our former discussions. Here it must be our first task to throw some light on the expression "to be of good will" which we have so frequently used.

In all ethical investigations a very clear distinction must be made between the following functions:—

1 (a) The intuition of the meaning of "good" in general, and in particular that of the good as actual intuition.

(b) The capacity for this intuition, which in some men is strong and in others weak, just as some men are good and others bad mathematicians.

2 (a) "Good" will—that is, the will which is turned upon the execution of that which in the individual instance has been intuited as being good.

(b) The capacity for such individual acts of good will.

3 (a) The good action—that is, the transformation of the individual act of good will into deed.

(b) The capacity for this. [It is true that here it may be said that, if the will mentioned under 2 (a) really is will, then the deed must follow of necessity. In this case 2 (b) and 3 (b) become one event.]

4 (a) The unchangeable general attitude of the will, whether it is the particular will mentioned under 2 or the deed which results from it.

(b) The capacity for this attitude.

We have here four times two concepts falling under various categories. The concepts of capacity are psychological concepts and denote the peculiarities of empirical psycho-physical beings. The other concepts—which are headed under (*a*)—denote facts of an actual kind: psycho-physical facts in the third instance and psychical facts in the others. (The first fact is, in modern terminology, "phenomenological".) These matters, however, are details; what is really important follows now.

The cases which we have enumerated do not necessarily occur together; this of course applies only to the "capacities". It is only too easy to find instances where they do not occur together—so easy, in fact, that it is almost possible to say that they occur together in no man. In theory we must admit that it is even possible that the fourth capacity does not exist—that is, the capacity for a general attitude of the will towards the good in will and deed. This is the only place where the expression "moral insanity" would be really appropriate; for surely it is part of the nature or health of a normal man that he possesses that general attitude of the Will, which, of course, implies that there is some intuition, however dim, of the meaning of good. We have no hesitation in asserting that this capacity is part of the nature of man: we shall, however, revert to this question.

Our tabulation now allows us to ascertain without difficulty the *homo bonae voluntatis*: that man possesses *bonam voluntatem* in perfection who has the capacity—4 (*b*)—to hold fast without restriction the general attitude of will towards the good in each particular instance. In a restricted sense we may predicate good will of those who will the good often but not always. We may also say that with these persons the general attitude of will towards the particular good volition is occasionally overcome by other impulses of will; for in principle we assert that this attitude—an attitude of the will in general towards the particular good will—is part of the "nature" of normal man.

All ethical propositions which refer to true duty and which are concrete are extremely "subjective"—that is, they are of an utterly personal nature. Hence it comes that we must use the greatest care in judging about the good will of another. His good will may be quite without restriction, and yet I may be blind to this fact because my highest aim has a different content from his, so that his aim, and consequently his actions, appear to me as ethically unsound.

This is continually happening in life. Here a man who has a real love and respect for his fellows will be able to find the right course. For example, a man whose convictions make him a pacifist will not ethically condemn as *homo malae voluntatis* a "militarist"; and so with a communist who judges a "nationalist" or even a "bourgeois": although in each case he will attempt to convert him to the acceptance of his own supreme standard of value.

5
ETHICAL JOY

We here reach an important question. How far is the ethical element connected with the element of happiness? We know that Kant attempts throughout to assert that there is no connection, although he cannot avoid making certain concessions. Here, too, we must make a distinction between the following terms: intuition of the good, particular good will, good action, and general good will to particular good will. We are not, of course, here dealing with the "capacities".

Now, in my view, it is impossible to deny that happiness does accompany the volitional event which tends to good will or good action in general, or that it accompanies the will to and execution of the individual good deed. The ethical intuition of good and of its realizations *as* ethical intuition alone may at best be called wholly disinterested; but in that case it must not be forgotten that every definitive intuition (for example, in geometry) is accompanied by a certain tinge of happiness.

We might even be tempted to say that the ethical will-event proper must have a tinge of happiness if only because without that tinge it would not be truly of a volitional nature. Of course the word "happiness" must not here be taken in any narrow or "sensual" sense. Its meaning cannot be defined; but it is not the same as the mere feeling of orderliness felt when something is approved as being *definitive*, which in a particular form is the main question everywhere in Ethics. In the "good man" the tinge of happiness attaches to that of approval. One might use the word "bliss" but that it has too religious a sound. The fact which we are describing is expressed by the words "It ought to be and I am glad that I can will it and do it." Let us then say "the tinge of joy", using it in no pharisaical but in a humble sense.

The "wholly good man", the "Saint" ("the beautiful soul") would in that case be the man who experiences this tinge of happiness only as attaching to the will to the good in general or in particular: he *can* will nothing but the good, whereas real man experiences happiness as attaching to will-contents which are ethically indifferent or even (unfortunately) wicked. This, of course, is not the note of happiness in the true sense.

No science has as many "-isms" as Ethics. All these are of an indefinite nature, at least if it is admitted that there is always happiness attaching to the good and that this is a particular form of joy.

If happiness in the good is the highest joy, then a general formal Ethics like that of Kant is hedonistic, even though it emphasizes that the proper motive for a truly ethical action must not consist in the anticipated joy of the impending happiness of conscience, but that the motive should be supplied by the object of the action. But implicitly such a system is eudaemonistic too, for its aim is that all men, if possible, shall enjoy that highest and truest happiness, the happiness in the good. It is even a utilitarian system, for to be good is for man, his nature being what it is, the greatest advantage. We are told, however, that the words "hedonistic", "eudaemonistic", "utilitarian" are meant to mean something entirely different.

Here we may ask a question. Was there ever a serious "Hedonist" who taught that mere personal pleasure (like pleasure in lasting bodily health, which is not of a merely fleeting kind) should be the moving force and aim of ethical action? Did ever a "Eudaemonist" teach the pleasure of all, or a "Utilitarian" the economic welfare of all, or at any rate of the greatest number?

I doubt it, even of the Epicureans. Possibly this has been taught by some modern cynics, and even by them only because they despaired to be able to realize their own profound intuition.

I think, then, that in principle and essentially all teachers of ethics are in agreement with regard to the foundation of ethics. The alleged divergences in the different schools, in my opinion, have a different source— one which refers to the ethical value to be attributed to the individual acts having a definite content. If this is correct, the differences between the opinions of the different schools are shifted from general ethics to applied ethics and from moral theory to practical philosophy proper. The latter, as we shall see, largely depends on metaphysical convictions.

At this place I confine myself to a few examples by way of explanation.

In a metaphysical sense a man may hold that the whole

of history, with its "progress", is indifferent; the true
goal of any supra-personal element may seem to him to
lie in the non-earthly, and humanity may seem a mere
stage in the non-earthly progress towards this goal. In
this progress it seems to him that he alone matters. It is
his conviction that he must care only to be good himself,
since in that way he better serves the highest, and with
it all mankind, than if he were to trouble about others
individually. Here again his conviction may follow two
distinct roads: the best means may be self-mortification
(St. Simeon), or again development of the personality
(Goethe).

This is no hedonism in the narrow sense of the word,
although in the highest sense it is hedonism and even
utilitarianism and eudaemonism. The ascetic remains
wholly centred upon himself, and shows no pity, for
precisely by this means both he and all other men are
"saved" magically so that thereby he and all have the
greatest joy and the greatest good. He is possessed by
the highest pity, and therefore has no pity for the things
of the earth.

The Goethe type is analogous; here the desire of
affording an example is of some importance.

The case is different for those to whom history, or at
any rate certain parts or aspects of history, are no more
than a series of earthly happenings. These do not believe
that they possess a mysterious power to save which is
peculiar to them, nor do they believe that they themselves
afford a perfect example to men. What they consider of

importance is the ethical work of many or even of all. Human society is not, indeed, an end to them, but it is a means of great importance, which accordingly is to be supported with all the strength at their disposal.

Here, however, we put an end to our examples, for at this point we are not really in a position properly to understand their significance.

All that they were here intended to show was that we must beware of assuming that the meaning of the postulate "it ought to be" is being apprehended in different manners when in fact the difference extended only to the content to which this postulate applies.

We saw that the true foundation of all ethics is not the genuine pity of one man for the other in the everyday sense. This is, however, invariably true of pity in the "highest sense". And this in turn is common to all ethical doctrines in some form, although often this is far from obvious. For it is the case that all moral doctrines are subordinate to that postulate which we formulated in an imperative form as the supreme demand of ethics, in so far as such doctrines are clear and earnest. There can be no ethics, and consequently there can be no particular moral doctrine, unless we assume some future supra-personal state which has been approved and is treated as our goal, whether it is the goal of an evolutionary process or not. This state is to be realized in a community of which the ethical subject is himself to be a member. This is as true as it is that there can be no mechanics without the concept of motion.

C

Fundamental divergences appear only at the point where it is necessary to determine in detail the meaning of Totality, Evolution, and Goal—that is, at the point where the individual ethical action has to be judged: in applied Ethics and moral doctrine.

6

DUTY AND FELLOWSHIP IN LIFE

We shall now proceed to some remarks upon Duty and Pity in their most universal and at the same time their highest forms—forms which, however, are also their vaguest and most neutral; for it is important to say that Duty and Pity in these their highest forms still belong to ethics as a theory of meanings, and must therefore be part of all ethical systems.

In order that the existence of ethical subjects shall be understood they must form part of a supra-personal order, and this order is the basis of their existence. It is here indifferent whether there is true "evolution" or not. Thus the content of their ethical intuition may relate to this order in two ways. First, every ethical subject in general is a member of the supra-personal order, and, secondly, each of these subjects is that particular member which it is.

Now that part of ethical consciousness which usually is called Pity is turned upon the general fact that a subject is a "member in general"—that is, that it is "man" (or, to an even wider view, that it is a living being). A better

name for Pity might be a "loving fellowship of life".[1]
It is at this point that the Christian concept of the *neighbour* comes into play.

Duty always refers to the fact that a subject is the particular member which he is; it is wholly personal, and is intuited in a manner which is valid for the individual alone. Scheler here rightly uses the expression, "that which is *absolutely* valid—for *me*".

Thus in every system of moral doctrine these two aspects of ethical intuition must find their practical fulfilment, and this is equally true whether the system is wholly turned towards, or away from, the earth. We already mentioned above that the ascetic who rises superior to all earthly pity is by this very fact practising pity in its highest form—by means of salvation. And those too who with Kant, Spinoza, and Nietzsche tend to despise pity are in fact exercising a higher pity, whether they demand that the man who has an inner fund of richness and strength shall show paternal benevolence towards the feeble, or that he shall be their guide, who is to lead them through a stage of suffering to a higher state. Even in a case where a man is cruel to his fellows and actually devotes some of them to death this generally is done from a conviction that in the highest sense a

---

[1] I here intentially confine myself to generalities, for these are sufficient for our purpose. The best treatment of this subject and all its branches will, of course, be found with Scheler, whether the distinctions which he makes are accepted or not; this applies even to his distinction between Spirit and Soul. It should be said, however, that we have in mind true pity and no sentimental infection. Cp. also Rehmke, *Grundlegung der Ethik als Wissenschaft*, 1925.

service is done thereby to other fellow-men (perhaps future men)—that is, to "members in general".

The categorical imperative in the form which Kant gave it applies to *fellowship in life*; here it is possible to speak of the demand for a universal law. This at any rate is true of the general form called "fellowship of life", although the content in which from time to time it manifests itself depends upon the manner in which the individual intuits his duty and upon his particular stock of knowledge.

On the other hand, the Kantian imperative is valid for *Duty* only in so far as the injunction to "do your duty" can be looked upon as the principle of a general law. But this assertion is perfectly void of content, for the concept of duty in general is as indeterminate as is the concept of figure in general in geometry: for a fellowship in life has a content which can be definitely stated, whereas duty in and for itself has not. Its content for each individual is what it is, and no individual can have knowledge of the content of the duty of another.

We remind the reader once more that the supreme principle of theoretical ethics is a proposition relating to the meaning of "it ought to be", whereas the supreme principle of practical moral doctrine may take the imperative form of "thou shalt" in a figurative form.

It is therefore possible to set up as the supreme principle of moral doctrine another and extremely general proposition: *That which has been accepted as good must be realized*. This proposition is an injunction which applies at once to fellowship of life and to general duty, and does not infringe upon the wholly personal nature of duty—that is to say, upon all that is particular in it.

7
THE PROBLEM OF APPLIED ETHICS

A. Its Metaphysical Foundation

It is the task of an applied Ethics and of a theory of morals based upon it, to investigate the particular forms in which love and duty must manifest themselves in order that they shall completely and definitively fulfil the concept of *good*—that is to say, in such a manner that nothing intuitable remains over that is not good.

It follows immediately from the concept of duty that such a doctrine can never be of completely universal validity, although it may be valid for the individual ego: it can be no more than a confession. And even with respect to the particular form in which love "ought" to be practised there can here be no more than a confession, at least with regard to ultimates, for we saw that the particular form in which a person clothes the manner in which he partakes of the fellowship in life is determined in part by his intuition of his duties. This is true, even though the bare term "fellowship in life" is not so poor in content as the bare term "duty", for the former term implies that in a certain sense all men (or living beings) are of equal rank, in so far as they are men (or living beings).

But now we reach a fact which is particularly weighty in rendering impossible any kind of perfectly universal validity of any moral doctrine.

We saw that the general content of every duty (and consequently the particular form of love) depends as far as its object is concerned upon the fact that it is in a relation to a final totality (goal) which is approved and which is the goal of the supra-personal evolution whose existence has been assumed in order that the existence of ethical subjects shall be intelligible. If the concept of evolution is rejected we may substitute a mere state in general—a state which is approved, is future, supra-personal, and whole, which is reached by a cumulative process but must not be imagined as an earthly state.

This final totality (or general state) is not given. We may only infer it—infer it metaphysically, for it is only upon a metaphysical foundation that ethical studies become more than a game in aesthetics.

Thus the standard against which the individual good is measured is hypothetical—it is a metaphysical hypothesis. This, so to speak, raises its inferential character to the second power, since metaphysics itself is no more than inference. First, then, the goal is inferred within the field of the doctrine of Order—that is, it is set up as a hypothesis upon a basis of fragmentary positive knowledge, and, secondly (since we are supposed to be dealing with metaphysics, and metaphysics cannot be dealt with otherwise than hypothetically), it is inferred that this inference, which itself is still of a logical nature, presents to us a particular actual state in a phenomenal manner.

Now it is true, of course, that it is possible to set up certain metaphysical propositions (for example, such as deal with the meaning of space) which are based upon the principle of manifoldness, if once it is admitted that the word "actual" has a meaning, and if it is assumed that it may be rationally applied. But such propositions are purely formal, or rather they belong to the theory of metaphysical relation. Of the nature of the actual we perceive only that knowledge in *some* form is appropriate to it.

There is no other part of metaphysics which has one sense only—that is, in all particular regions of metaphysics it is possible to posit more than one assertion, all which equally imply the positing of that which is known as "appearance", and would thus serve to explain appearance. This is especially true of the higher ontology, which stands close to the problem of Death; and more particularly of the metaphysics of the supra-personal final totality, for it is this which allowed us to have a glimpse of what may be called the higher stages of ontology, the approach to which lies through the problem of death.

Now, a moral doctrine which has its basis in concrete ethics must have the whole or part of its foundation in precisely these facts, as will soon appear.

Perhaps our own statement will here be used to refute us—our statement to the effect that in certain empirical instances the meaning of good can be intuited in an absolute manner; and it may be said that this settles the case. But when we intuit "it ought to be" we do so in a perfectly indefinite manner, just as I can apprehend "depth" in a perfectly indefinite manner, but must have resort to measurement if I want to obtain a definite depth.

We now ask whether after all there are not any further and more satisfactory facts which might render the term "good" rather less colourless.

B. ARE THERE PARTICULAR MORAL FEELINGS?

This brings us to a new and fundamental question which was adumbrated in the statement that the inferred goal (which is the standard to which the *good* in general is related) must be approved.

What is the meaning of Kant's Categorical Imperative? It tells us that an action is good if I can desire that the underlying maxim could be made the principle of a universal law. The question then arises, What universal standard can I here desiderate, and what do I desiderate? The answer is, A maxim which is good. It is good, and therefore I desiderate it as the principle underlying a law. Thus I define "good" by means of a sentence which does not become intelligible until we know the meaning of "good".

Our own formulation of the imperative is not in much better case. Why do I approve a future state which is to be reached by means of a process either of evolution or of cumulation, which is to serve for standard of the good? I approve it because it would be good.

If we are told that an action is good if it represents an attempt at the realization of some value, then our next question is, Under what conditions does something become a "value" in the ethical sense. The only possible answer in this case is: If it is considered to be a value by somebody who is *good*.

There remains another formulation: "Do to another as he wishes you to do." Perhaps this may turn out to be a form of the ethical law which, though popular, is correct. Certainly it would be so—that is, if the other wills the good. Or we might say: "Do to others as you would have them do to you." Certainly—if that which you would have done to yourself is good. Again: What would a community of saints be? We might answer: A community which realizes the harmonious adjustment of all wills to one another. True—but only on the assumption that all the wills are good. Thus it appears that we are still moving in a circle. Perhaps we are explaining, but we are certainly not defining.

More than this, however, we cannot do; for such meanings as "it ought to be" or "good" are fundamental. I am aware intuitively when they are fulfilled, although I cannot account to myself for the fact that in the individual case I judge that they are fulfilled. All that can be said about the meaning of "good" is that it is something definitive with respect to *order* within the sphere of something that in some way is of the nature of a totality.

We said above that ethical intuition is a kind of instinct. It is true that the intuition which we had in mind had for object a *form* of order of a very general nature, as we emphasized a few lines above; and in this sense it is possible, of course, to call all the forms in which order is intuited instinctive, as soon as we leave the egocentric standpoint of the doctrine of order and pass over to the psychological point of view. In that event we may say that there are psycho-physical human persons, and that there exists a multiplicity of these, and, further, that a potential knowledge of the greater forms in which order is applied to the world is inborn or immanent in them, and that in order that it shall become real it requires stimulation coming from empirical experience.

At this point, however, we have something wholly different in mind. Here we are taking the word "instinct" in the more definite and narrower sense which it has in biology and animal psychology. Here it does no harm if we assume the naïvely realistic standpoint, provided that it is settled once and for all that it is a naïvely realistic standpoint, and that we are aware of its significance within the strict doctrine of order.

Here, then, "instinct" means an innate and actual knowledge about particular empirical facts with respect to their essential content. Instinct becomes a feeling of a cognitive nature, to use the expression coined by Scheler, although we would here prefer not to make use of the term "feeling", since it denotes a mere empirical addition, as also it does in the expression "feeling of evidentness". We have, in fact, here an intuition of significances (which is accompanied by a note of feeling), just as much as we have one when we intuit the law of the excluded middle or a geometrical axiom.

From a certain period in its life onwards the Weaver Bird knows what a nest is, and the bee knows what a comb is, although their knowledge has not the form of our knowledge. Next, these creatures "will" the existence of nest or comb, the nature of which they had previously merely "dreamed", as the old school of natural philosophers aptly used to say. It is true that the final execution of that which is willed takes place in a manner different from that in which man wills and executes something after some empirical experience has gone before. For man is forced to experiment, whereas creatures of instinct have innate in them, together with the goal of their volitions, a definitive knowledge about the one and only correct means to that end. Similarly, the Entelechy of Form possesses "primary knowledge and volition" with regard to the necessary steps, without any experiment. (This is the case, for example, where Regeneration takes place.)

We now ask whether man as a psycho-physical being has a similar innate intuitive knowledge about matters of moral theory. Such knowledge would be something more than systems of formal relations. In what could such knowledge consist? Does he ever intuit the meaning of "good" in some particular event, which thereafter he intuits in its particular nature to be good *a priori*, just as the meaning of "beside" is invariably apprehended in certain particular manifestations of space? If such an intuitive knowledge about particular instances of good existed, then evidently it would be expressed in the consciousness of the ego—that strange entity which stands above unity and multiplicity. (In using this term we are for a moment taking up the strict standpoint of the doctrine of order which takes solipsism as its method.) I would then intuit *a priori*—that is, in a manner independent of empirical quantum and not admitting of subsequent correction, that here, and in precisely these contents, I am in the presence of good or evil. This intuition would accompany certain particular empirical experiences, and the first intuition would suffice for all time. It is true that a subject—to revert to psychological terminology—need not know, so to speak, explicitly what this means: he need not know that in this instance he is having instinctive knowledge of good or evil, nor need he know what this implies, any more than natural man has knowledge of parallel lines, or knows what this implies. It is possible even that in man instinct has the conscious form of a mere impulse or of an urge—of a tendency, or of a dim intuition of the fact that there must be a something whose nature it is to fulfil a certain wish, to be found in a certain direction. But still the nature of the case would be such that, if an initiated person were to inform the subject of the meaning of knowledge about particular instances of good or evil, the subject would reply that he had suspected it all along, but that he had not had a clear notion up to this moment about this knowledge of good or evil particularities (or of parallel lines) and of the ultimate significance of this knowledge in terms of the theory of Order.

We need not demonstrate in detail the enormous importance for a scientific system of concrete Ethics, and for a moral theory, of an instinctive knowledge about particular ethical events, even if the number of particular instances to which this knowledge related was very small. It is true that a moral theory would not even then attain absolute validity, since it is the nature of duty to be utterly personal. But in part at least it would be "scientific" in the sense that it would be final for the ego, and precisely this part would attain a practically universal validity, which otherwise it could in no sense attain. At length it would become possible to pass beyond that unprogressive ethical formalism in which critical ethics has been held fast since the time of Kant.

Ethics must at least make the attempt to answer the question what ought to be done in each individual instance in accordance with its particular content, and why the course which is, in fact, adopted ought to be adopted to the exclusion of all others. Kant's Imperative is wholly inadequate to the solution of this problem.

In this section we do not propose to answer the question whether there is an instinctive knowledge of particular ethical facts which is immediate and intuitive, and how wide is its scope. Here we will merely say that in any case it does not go very far. Hence that which in the narrower sense is of instinctive nature requires for complement that analytical reflection about certain positive pieces of knowledge shall be added. This reflection relates to an incomplete and supra-personal evolution towards an approved goal x, or at any rate towards an approved future *total* state; it takes place within the sphere of metaphysics and therefore must at best be "hypothetical", as we know already, in a double sense. But at least we now see that a moral theory is possible which is composed in part of hypothetical elements, and in part of such as are definitive for the ego, and therefore are in practice of universal validity, and, so to say, are of instinctive nature.

The instinctive or *a priori* element in this theory relates to the note of approval of the goal as well of the individual action. The hypothetical metaphysical element relates to the actual nature of the goal and of particulars. Here if it is hypothetically possible that there is more than one goal, those which cannot be approved are immediately rejected, and if it is allowed that there can be degrees of approval, these degrees play an active part when the hypotheses are formed, so that in the end we must admit that the ultimate goal of all action is determined when one course is approved above all others.

C. The Danger of Feelings Due to Habit

The only instincts which are of the nature of feelings and of a cognitive nature, and of which we can really admit that they are important for concrete Ethics, are such as are truly *a priori* from their origin, or at any rate have a kernel which from its origin is *a priori*.

For there also exist habitual feelings which are the results of early training, and these even constitute the ambient atmosphere for the ordinary man, who thinks that they are cognitive. This applies to every kind of politics which makes an appeal to the feelings. From his earliest days it has been implanted in a man that a certain institution or line of action or person is "excellent", "praiseworthy", "brave", or "contemptible". There are many such catchwords. When these sentiments were implanted in him they were always accompanied by a definite note of feeling, and this has "infected' him, or, to use the terminology of the psychiatrist, has created a complex. Thus the idea of these men or actions is always accompanied in him by a note of feeling in either a positive or a negative sense, and the result is that he thinks that he has an "innate" feeling which affords him knowledge about that which ought and that which ought not to be. The truth is that he has no knowledge at all, and that in fact he has been hindered in attaining knowledge whether of a hypothetical or an intuitive kind.

All the great teachers of morals have had to wage a war against the presumption of habitual feelings, and we too will be faced by this task. Sometimes there is a true original instinctive intuition at the bottom of an habitual feeling, and in that case there is a certain justification for the feeling. We shall find that in such cases it is particularly difficult to separate the chaff from the grain and to winnow it away.

But even if it is true that there are occasions when habitual feelings possess a certain original and *a priori* foundation their most essential foundation always is egoism in one form or another, an egoism which often is no more than laziness and hides behind a bulwark of herd-feeling. It will appear that this is true, for example, of a certain type of "patriotism".

Here Ethics must ruthlessly eradicate the weeds. But it must not allow itself to be deterred by this great difficulty in its search after genuine cognitive instincts which are of the nature of feelings.

8

THAT WHICH OUGHT TO BE AND THAT WHICH IS

We may here briefly mention a question which in these days is often debated *ad nauseum*—the question about the relation which subsists between that which ought to be and that which is.

It goes without saying that that which is is not the index of that which ought to be; for the very meaning of "ought" implies that that which ought to be in fact is not.

Now, it is true that we have placed the foundations of Ethics in hypothetical metaphysical knowledge, save only in so far as we are dealing with the apriority of particular contents. It looks as though this were a more subtle instance of the relation between *ought* and *is*, and such in fact it is in two respects.

In the first place we are attempting to postulate the existence of a supra-personal entity in order to obtain a metaphysical explanation for the existence of ethical subjects (but not of the actual content of the good). The subjects are part of the entity and as such are irradiated by it.

This is the metaphysical reading of the fact which is expressed by the words: "There are subjects having ethical intuition", and, as has already been said, it has nothing to do with the content of the given good.

In the second place, we hold that considerations dealing with a real Existence may well determine the *direction* of statements which deal with the contents of ethics. In this case, that which ought to be is derived from that which is. It is not, however, derived from that which is empirically. We have just uttered a warning against any over-estimation of feelings which we find existing within us, since it is possible that these are no more than habitual feelings implanted by education. We do not mean that which has empirical existence, but that whose essence it is to *be*. We have in mind such questions as the meaning of life and of death.

We form hypotheses with regard to these, and in

doubtful cases (that is, where immediate cognitive instinct fails us) such hypotheses with regard to the essence of things may play a directive part for particular ethical judgments. Here a relation is established between eternal Being or essential Being, so to say, and ethical Being.

Now, in a certain respect it must be true even of empirical Being that a man's ethical field of action will be richer, and his ethical intuition more subtle, as his empirical knowledge, especially in so far as it relates to social entities, grows wider. Unless I know empirically what breath, child, and water *are*, I cannot save a child from drowning.

Thus all that is not permissible is, to infer what ought to be from individual empirical events. It is precisely this fault which is committed by so many teachers of ethics who deal in feelings.

9

CONSPECTUS OF THE FUNDAMENTAL CONCEPTS OF ETHICS, WITH A TERMINOLOGY BASED UPON "VALUE"

This is the place where we may well make some remarks upon the relation between an instinctive knowledge of ethical particularities and of the content of the supreme goal on the one hand, and the general intuition having the abstract form "it ought to be" on the other hand. In doing this we shall make use of a term which is enjoying a good deal of popularity in these days.

We shall make use of the term "value" which since the time of Lotze and Nietzsche has found a place in modern philosophy, although its ambiguity makes it rather distasteful to us. To begin with, we shall say something about the different meanings which are actually to be found.[1]

The term "value" has been used by different authors in the following senses:—

Firstly, the final state of a series of events which is approved (that is to say, of which it is judged that it ought to be), where the events are actually happening empirically, whether this process is a true evolution or not.

Secondly, any means which serves to attain this.

Thirdly, the goal of any volition, where this goal is "subjectively" held to be final.

Fourthly, any means to its attainment which is "subjectively" held to be suitable.

[1] Cp. K. Wiederhold, *Wertbegriff und Wertphilosophie*, Kantstudien, Supplementary No. 52, 1920. J. E. Heyde, too (Kantstudien, 31, 1926, and *Wert*, Erfurt, 1926), is aware of the confusion which exists in this matter and seeks to clear it up: A beautiful vase has value, a beautiful vase is a value, the beauty of a vase is a value, etc. Heyde rightly rejects the platonic "existence" of values. They always require a something in which they exist, although, like numbers and forms, they can also be considered as independent meanings. He also rightly emphasizes, as against Scheler, that the apprehension of a value is always accompanied with a note of pleasure. (*Wert*, pp. 111, 117, etc.) But Heyde makes no distinction between values which are means and hence are states, and means which are values and are events. In my opinion too, where he speaks of relations the distinction between subjective and objective relations is not made perfectly clear. They all are frequently related to the ego, in so far as they are experienced (or are possessed in a conscious manner); but often it looks as though Heyde (e.g. p. 153) saw no more than this relation: he gives the name of value to a relation between valuable object and feeling of value; this is inadequate.

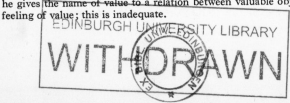

"Value" is a relation only in the second and fourth instances, although of course every kind of "value" falls within the fundamental relation "I consciously possess something".

Fifthly, we must mention the concept of value as used in Economics, where it simply denotes the equivalent of money.

For the time being we will confine ourselves to the so-called "subjective" meanings. Here "subjective" denotes something which expressly is looked at as belonging to the consciousness of the ego in the shape of an object (or, as experienced). In that case we now suggest the following set of concepts.

Absolute value, or final value, or value as such. This is a schematic concept, or, in my own terminology, an "anticipated scheme" of such a kind that after its objective realization everything would be final, and volition would have no further aim, except indeed the preservation of the state of realization.

Partial or auxiliary value. This is an imaginary schematic state on the road to the realization of the final value, the realization of which as such can be willed more particularly. If this value falls within the category of the ethical, it is called good.

Means towards value. This is the name of every event which consciously serves the realization of the absolute value or of a partial value. If this Means more particularly serves the realization of that partial value which is called the ethical partial value, then it is called good.

Thus we give the name of value only to states: events which stand in some relation to value we call means towards a value. The latter alone are relations of a dynamic nature, whereas auxiliary values are logical relationships. Absolute value is unrelated. All these things, of course, are experienced, and as such fall under the description "I consciously experience something".

For man according to his essence absolute value is to behold order perfectly fulfilled—that is to say, to see everything as being in a state of order so that nothing remains over to ask or to be desired.

Among many others there is one partial value which in turn is divided up into many subordinate partial values: this value is, to intuit order in the community of men, or the realization of morality, this intuition being considered as a state. This also applies to the will to realize a certain order, as a state.

To tell the truth, or to teach ethics by example, is a means towards value—a good means towards a value, according to our definition. Ethical theory, on the other hand, as ethical theory, is of course not good in any sense, although it is a partial value—that is, a stage on the way to the realization of the supreme value. This is true also of the theory of mechanics.

The will to the realization of the partial value, "to intuit morality", is, as we know, part of the nature (*essentia*) of man, unless he is suffering from moral insanity; and it, as well as the general or particular will to a good action (p. 26), is not a means towards a value in our terminology, but a value which is a means, or a partial value, forming part of morality in general, which is itself a value of this kind: for here we are dealing with states. Thus the "good man", held to be such by reason of his disposition, is a state, and therefore is a value which is a means. His good actions are means towards a value.

It will not be easy to avoid the ambiguity of the word "good" without doing violence to language, so common are the expressions "good man" and "good deed".

A classification of partial values and of means towards values is discovered in the course of an investigation of the problems which are connected with the concept of Order; and that means, of all problems whatever, since a *problem* is the same thing as a *question* within the scope of the concept of Order. As far as ethical problems are concerned this classification will be given by us implicitly in the course of the following pages, although we shall refrain from using the term "value", which we used on this one occasion simply in order to establish relations with other theories.

It is clear that such a classification must be genuine, and must contain a system of superior and inferior categories. A mere enumeration cannot be definitive. For example, although Spranger's ideal human types based upon values simply stand side by side, this is probably no more than a temporary arrangement, and, besides, they are all subordinated to a supreme value, which according to Spranger is the ethical value. This kind of system is genuinely based upon classification, and it seems to me that here more use might be made of meta-physical hypotheses based upon knowledge of empirical facts than is made by Scheler, who makes the formation of systems a matter of immediate intuition.

The absolute value, all partial values, and all means towards values are, within the general doctrine of order, meanings which belong to some ego, that is, they are objects in the most general sense—a sense which, however, does not include platonic realism. Everything, in so far as it has a meaning, is here intuited as existing, so that it stands on the same footing as such meanings as "so much", "reason", "triangle", etc.[1] Once the concept of the "other ego" has been introduced into the doctrine of Order, no matter how, and once this concept and that of the soul have been used as the foundation of psychology, the intuition of values is part of the *essence* of the intuiting egoes and souls. Thus values and the means towards values now exist, but they do so only in so far as the souls and egoes exist which own them. Thus they now have a second objective—existence in harmonious co-ordination to their subjective existence. This existence is tied to the existence of souls, while the other or objective existence consists in the fact that they are particularities in certain states or events, in exactly the same way as meanings like "so much", "reason", "triangle" exist in an objective and empirical manner in certain empirical states which so to speak they saturate. We may call these

---

[1] Heyde (*Wert*, pp. 63, 145) justly notes that values are found empirically and are not made.

the bearers of values, and may thus distinguish between them and values, where the latter are treated as meanings; but before doing so we must consider that the track of a comet may equally well be called the bearer of a parabola, and a causal relationship, the bearer of reasons. Nothing much would be gained by such a procedure.

It is true that, in that part of the doctrine of Order which deals with the soul and nature, souls and the events of nature exist only as quasi-independent. In metaphysics, however, each such quasi-independent entity is given its absolute correlative. Once this has been brought about there is such a thing as objective intuition of value, and, harmoniously co-ordinated with it, there is objective realization of values. There are objective entities in harmonious correspondence with intuition which is *a priori* and subjective. In other words, there are empirical contents to which I can apply (so to speak) value-concepts which I have intuited *a priori*. We may here compare the relation which subsists between geometry and physics.

It is much to be desired that an end were made of all that so-called platonism which in fact is not platonism at all; for Plato was naïve enough to think of his realm of ideas as something metaphysical. This is an advantage, however, compared with modern indefiniteness; for at any rate his meaning is clear.

On the other hand, it is anything but clear what is the meaning of the modern "true propositions in themselves", "absolute validities", or "composite meanings", our "universal validities", our "self-warranting truths".

No man has yet succeeded in explaining the meaning of such expressions as these, not even the "phenomeno-logists".

There are meanings and complexes of meanings which I experience, and this experience is accompanied by a note of definitiveness, or of order. These notes tell me "this is complete", "this is in order", or "there is nothing to be altered here". Such notes are characteristic of value-meanings.

An experienced content may, then, have definitiveness; but it can have universal validity at most in the empirical sense—that is, validity for all empirically existing subjects. Existence here means, to be the object of experience.

The fact that *I experience something* is indivisible; it is triune. It is also a part of this fact that a something is saturated with order-notes of a particular kind.

Thus the so-called "being" of every definitive fact is always attached to a personal experience.

The case is altered, as has already been stated, in the sphere of metaphysics. Here there are many knowing subjects. But that which is of the nature of a meaning "exists" even here only in so far as is attached to these.

That which really *is*, is in its actuality, which has being and is saturated with meaning. But the question arises whether we can attribute any existence to meaning as such. To me the implied assertion is meaningless. It seems to me that here the wish has been father to the alleged thought. We would like to have something that is abso-lute and universally valid, and we will not be satisfied with the fact that all we can have is, first, definitive knowledge relating to mere empirical meanings, and, secondly, hypothetical knowledge of that which is.

Those who call this a merely psychological doctrine know little of the nature of psychology and of its potentialities. Often enough a caricature of psychology is made up in order that "universal validity" may shine in greater brightness—a brightness of the footlights.

It will not be disputed that the introduction of the term "value" brought with it a great deal of confusion in philosophy. Not only is it the case that different meanings were attached by different thinkers to this word, but even the same thinker gives to it different meanings—sometimes that of a state and sometimes that of an event—without warning the reader, and often without noticing it himself. It is especially important, in our opinion, to decide definitely whether the last term in a series is to be called a value, or whether we will give this name to something which allows this last term to be realized. It is clear that in such a case there will always be a note of finality, to use our own phraseology. When we pass from theoretical intuition to practical injunction this note may be called a *rule*, and it is this note which is the indefinable part in value. But, apart from this, values are quite easy to define, for a value is a rather composite thing. We have already discussed objectivity and subjectivity, but here, in order to avoid confusion, we say once more that the only meaning of subjective can be that an entity is the object of the experience of egoes which are quasi-independent or genuinely independent—that is, that it is object in the widest sense. Objective, on the other hand, means that that of which objectivity is predicated exists as a realized note in states or events which, apparently or really, exist for themselves. Once more we offer an example: I experience such *meanings* as "parallel" or "parabola", etc., and there exist what are at any rate approximations of parallel lines and parabolae. I experience $2 + 2 = 4$, which is a complex of meanings, and there exist two dogs and again two dogs—that is, four dogs.

Value-meanings, then, are composite objects of experience, and the *definitive* element is always a part of them. Thus these meanings can be intuited purely as meanings, and also as imbedded, so to say, in empirical reality, and as saturating it.

10

THE PROBLEM OF CONCRETE ETHICS FURTHER CONSIDERED

From now onward we shall use the word "value" only occasionally in discussing the question (to which we now revert) as to the relation which subsists between particular cognitive ethical intuitions and the general intuition which informs us that "this ought to be".

General ethical intuition is itself a particular instance of the most universal kind of intuition of order. Its results are framed in a purely abstract manner in the formulae *ethical value in general* ("it ought to be") and *ethical means towards value in general* ("good action"). General ethical intuition cannot give us more than this—that is (in our own terminology), more than subjective definitiveness with respect to the supra-personal objective totality and to the means by which it may be reached.

It is at this point that particular "instinctive" ethical intuition might become operative and might manifest itself in approval. It might determine the ethical value in general in a particular manner in accordance with its particular manifestation; which particular determination might not perhaps be an ultimate goal, but might be an intermediate state—that is, the means by which the goal is to be reached. Perhaps in this manner, too, it might succeed in analysing into subordinate partial values the genus "ethical value", which, relatively to the supreme value, is itself no more than a partial value.

In a certain sense, of course, this analysis does take place within the sphere of general ethical intuition, for this intuition allows us to separate duty from community in life, although both of these still remain entirely formal. Community in life really is an over-statement; the concept with which we are really dealing is that of being a member of a whole.

But perhaps the genuine particular "cognitive" moral instinct could tell us better than anything else how this community is to be practised, and what is the meaning of duty. Perhaps it might even tell us whether this practice is in the strict sense desirable or not.

In other words, the ethical fundamental intuition "this ought to be" allows us to go "beyond the person to definitiveness", but it does not allow more than this.

Thus it appears that general ethics in its more narrow and peculiar sense is not yet concerned with community of life, or sorrow, or joy, or with love, or whatever other means there may be (according to Scheler) that can lead us "beyond the person to definitiveness". These are the concern of particular applied ethics, and hence of moral doctrine.

Now, at this point we are searching after particular cognitive instincts. That which they tell us must, of course, always fall under the general category of the "it ought to be"—that is to say, the category of ethical value or supra-personal definitiveness. Scheler particularly emphasized the fact that circumstances can arise when it may be perfectly unethical to share in somebody's pleasure, where such pleasure means participation in pleasure in something non-moral. This fact is here definitely settled in a positive sense.

But in our opinion particular ethical instincts would be something remarkable because (as it seems to me) they would be the sole instance in man of *a priori* knowledge of a particular kind referring to empirical facts. They would not be a genuinely apprehending instinct, but they would still be more than impulses manifesting themselves subjectively in restlessness and the like, and therein they would differ from all other so-called human instincts.

Particular moral instincts would then be something very remarkable. They would not consist in the faculty of having *a priori* knowledge of particular empirical facts, and they would consist in the faculty of immediately apprehending the note of ethical definiteness (of definitiveness related to a totality), provided that such facts were consciously possessed and understood.

Scheler admits such an apprehension of definiteness in the phenomenological apprehension of that which, precisely, he calls values and classifies. But this does not help him beyond Kant's formalism. We, however, cannot follow him in his platonic realism, and we are, further, of the opinion that he admits far too much as unanalysable "quality", as he calls it. We know already that in the investigation of that which is really unanalysable very great caution is required, for there are such things as feelings of habit. Why precisely there are these elementary values is a question which evidently must have an answer, and the only possible answer must be a hypothetical and metaphysical one. Scheler does not answer this question, but just simply posits his values.

If there were such a thing as "cognitive" ethical intuition, then, of course, like everything else that partakes of the nature of a category, it would be a particular instance of that harmony which subsists between the subjective and the objective side of reality. We have discussed this at another place.[1]

The last point of reference of all applied ethics is, as

[1] Driesch, *Wirklichkeitslehre*. Second edition, 1922, pp. 235 *sqq.*

it has always been, the highest objective ethical value—
that is, that state of spiritual mankind in which, if it
were to be realized, everything would be in *order* with
respect to mankind. The only form in which I can intuit
this state (as subjective highest ethical value) is that of
an approved schematic structure. It can be filled in only
by means of metaphysical hypotheses. We have already
pointed out that the setting up of these hypotheses is
always accompanied by the view that they are "good"
and "approved". Thus, as has always rightly been
asserted, "ought" cannot be derived from "is", for if
this were the case the "goal" would necessarily be bad
in times of obvious ethical and intellectual decadence.
But it must be possible to say that that which ought to
be might be *potentially*; and to be acquainted with
potential Being is a part of ontology, which within the
sphere of metaphysics is hypothetical.

Thus empirical data are ultimately the basis upon
which are founded all metaphysical hypotheses which
seek to establish Ethics intellectually. They are the
foundation of all the rest of metaphysics, and they consist
in part of the contents of knowledge (whether it has
physical, psycho-physical, or psychological facts for
object), and in part in immediate "instinctive" intuitions.

A permanent reciprocal relation subsists between instinctive intuitions and metaphysical hypotheses in so far
as the intuitions help in the formation of the hypotheses,
while the hypotheses render intelligible the contents of
intuition in their empirical presentation.

If we give the name of deliverance to the highest approved ethical state, then deliverance is the ultimate end of every ethical act. At the beginning, of course, it is left open what is to be the meaning of deliverance. It may mean the destruction of empirical actuality (or of its absolute substratum), or the overcoming of dualism within the system of the world in an infinite progress, and it may be given still other meanings.

In so far as ethics makes *deliverance* its *summum bonum* and point of reference, it operates with the one fundamental principle: "There ought to be deliverance." But this one principle cannot provide ethics with any new views. It will have to attempt to set up fundamental particular axioms each of which must, of course, imply the positing of the highest principle.

II

THE ETHICAL AXIOM

Thus a systematic applied Ethics and Moral Theory would have to begin from elementary propositions which had been immediately intuited as being "self-evident" (axioms), exactly like systematic geometry. It would have to develop its particular theorems within the structure of a framework (the nature of which is indicated by the word "good"), beginning from axioms and relying upon constructions, which in turn are based upon definitions.

In such a system of ethics empirical facts (like physical facts in a system of geometry) would be a stimulus towards the development of fresh constructions which *might* have been discovered even without this stimulus. For it would be the task of applied Ethics and of Moral Theory to deal with the whole of potentiality within the category of good and evil (it being understood that these two terms refer to empirical actuality), just as geometry should and does deal with the whole of potentiality within the category of space. It is possible, after all, to assert the potentiality of an event anywhere within empirical actuality; for example, within the theory of causality.[1]

These considerations lead us to a guiding principle which will prove extremely important for all that is to follow: "No particular theorem in any complete systematic moral theory should ever contradict any of its axioms"; just as in geometry no theorem may be in conflict with the principle that similar triangles have their angles equal. Indeed, this guiding principle of ours ought really to apply in a moral theory in which there are no genuine axioms at all (that is, axioms which have been intuited originally to be definitive), but only hypothetical axioms—axioms which really are no axioms. Once such pseudo-axioms have been posited they are valid, even though the positing was an arbitrary act.

As far as I know almost all the authors of ethical systems have failed to observe this principle. Perhaps the failure has been smallest with the Indian ethical systems, and the ethical system of the Sermon of the Mount and of Tolstoy.

[1] Cp. Driesch, *Ordnungslehre*. Second edition, 1923, pp. 197 *sqq.*

If we wish to give an exact logical formulation to the principle that subsequent theorems of ethics must not be in conflict with axiomatic or pseudo-axiomatic principles, we reach the following conclusion.

Ethical principles may be divided into two classes: into prohibitions and commandments (to put it practically) or into propositions having the form "it ought not to be" or "it ought to be" (to put it in a purely theoretical manner). (In the terminology of the theory of freedom—(p. 23 *sq*.)—this would be expressed thus: into instructions which tell me when I must assent to, and when I must dissent from, the contents of my will.)

Elementary propositions having a negative form exercise a binding force upon all that follows, inasmuch as none of the later propositions may contain anything that is covered by the application of the prohibition. Thus if any potential action implies something that is prohibited by an axiom or a pseudo-axiom, then this suffices to prohibit the action in principle and once and for all. Positive elementary propositions, on the other hand, must be preserved in the subsequent propositions in two ways: (1) No subsequent particular proposition may contain any part that implies the negation of any positive elementary proposition; and (2) if it is valid for the same particular region as some elementary proposition, it must contain this latter. This does not tell us what is enunciated by the particular ethical proposition.

The reason for this is that the negative elementary propositions are, from the logical point of view, consequences of which it is negated that they "ought" to be. Thus here it is true that the negation of the consequence implies the negation of each of its possible reasons, and this truth applies to the particular category of ought. The positive elementary propositions are such consequences as have received assent. In ordinary logic a consequence to which assent has been given does not tell us anything definite about the possible reason from which it follows. But at least it tells us this much about it—that the negation of the consequence to which assent has been given cannot follow from it, and that the consequence, on the other hand, must follow from it. In this way the logic of commandments and that of prohibitions is reduced to the common logic of the implications which follow from the contents of the subject.

From what has been said it follows that ethical prohibitions are unequivocal, which is more than can be said of ethical commandments. Perhaps this is one of the reasons why they predominate in all ethical systems. Another of these reasons has been discussed by me in the theory of freedom.[1]

12

THE ETHICAL PROBLEM AS RESTRICTED TO THE REAL

We know that our moral theory might deal with mere "potentialities" falling within the frame of certain

[1] *Grundprobleme der Psychologie*, 1926, p. 229.

empirical actualities. However, now that we are proceeding to its practical application we will confine it to actually existing events.

Accordingly we presuppose that there is empirical knowledge about all the facts which are relevant to the matter—that is, a knowledge the objects of which are the facts of the soul, of sociology, of nature, and so forth. It is true that sociology as such is an empirical science, and deals with facts. It merely furnishes us with material, and the peculiar "it ought to be" plays no part in it in any circumstances. What we are here concerned with is the moral judging of sociological facts (or the relating of them to a standard of value, as the popular expression goes); and this is a wholly different matter. Max Weber used rightly to lay particular stress upon this fact.

In what circumstances might I call my own actions and those of others good? This, as we know, is the first question which we have to investigate. Now an individual action is never simply and merely good or bad: these predicates apply to it only in so far as it is a particular action relating to a particular empirical actuality. Now if here we were to start from the concept of empirical actuality and to consider everything that was *a priori* possible under this category (like the course of action to adopt with regard to ghosts or to angels) from the ethical point of view, this would not be thoroughness but pedantry; and this would be true in spite of the fact that we are well aware once and for all that an action *ought to be*, not because in fact it deals with empirical facts, but because, within this particular category of the empirical, it is one case among the multiplicity of potential empirical cases, and, being such, also happens to be good.

Thus we proceed immediately to our applied ethics from our positive empirical knowledge about the actual facts of reality: such as that there is organic and inorganic matter, there are men and beasts, men and women, children, poor, sound, and sick, and so forth.

But it is true that all this in strictness is ethically contingent.

THE DOCTRINE OF DUTIES

I

WE HAVE NO DUTIES TOWARDS THE NON-LIVING

No moral obligations exist towards the non-living as such.

We will make this proposition the beginning of our attempt at setting up a moral theory based upon applied ethics. Its definitive nature is clear immediately once the nature of the concept "ought to be" has been intuited. This concept always refers to something which in turn is referred to some totality, and which (1) forms part of the contents of some conscious entity, and (2) is realized with certainty only within the realm of the living.

It is true that a certain hypothetical element attaches even to this our negative proposition, since we cannot know with complete certainty that that which we call non-living is not a part of some living totality which is supra-personal and unknown to us.

But we are not obliged to assert that this our proposition is an axiom. It is designed merely to set a limit to our task.

If we insist upon casting it in an axiomatic form we must say that if there is something non-living in the strict sense, then no moral obligation exists towards it as such.

Careful note must be made of the words "as such".

By these words we wish to make it clear that our proposition does not settle anything about our attitude towards the non-living in so far as the latter stands in some relation or other to the non-non-living. A statue is non-living, but a twofold relation subsists between it and the living: it is the work of men, and it acts upon men in a cheering or an edifying manner. A tract of country, too, although it is not the work of men, can be in an active relation to men; thus deposits of coal and of iron ore may be of economic value, although at the given moment they may be inert.

Such things, then, are not "non-living as such", and our proposition is very far from expressing ethical indifference towards them. It might even be doubted whether there is anything "non-living as such" in the strictest sense—quite apart from the question which has already been raised whether that which we consider non-living is so in fact in and for itself.

2

DUTIES TOWARDS "MY" PERSON

It has for long been the custom to speak of a man's duties towards himself and of his duties towards others, where his attitude towards living entities comes into question. Probably the word "duty" was here understood, not in our narrower sense, which limits this concept so as to exclude community in the life of another entity, but merely as an abbreviated form of "it ought to be" in general.

It is certain that this traditional classification of duties is roughly correct. But it must be defined more narrowly, and the classification must be carried farther.

For the words "towards myself" we must substitute "towards my psycho-physical person"; for by *I* we mean simply the pure point of reference of conscious experience and nothing farther. If we make this verbal change we recognize immediately that it is possible to undertake a division of the person, and hence of my duties towards it, in so far as I am dealing with my person. For I am dealing, first, with that unique natural fact which is called my body; and, secondly, there is my soul.

With respect to that which is "mine" it is certain that a careful distinction must be made between these two. It remains to be seen later whether this is necessary with respect to "others" also.

A. Duties Towards My Body

We will proceed, then, to speak of the duties towards my body.

If the question of duty arises here at all, it does so in our sense; for the concept of a sharing in life, in sensation, or in suffering becomes meaningless where "I" (to use the popular term) am the only person concerned.

First, then, my body lives, and, secondly, it is the

instrument of my soul. (The meaning of this may be interpreted at will.)

Thus it is possible to speak of duties towards the body as a living entity in general, and of duties towards it as an instrument of the soul.

(*a*) MY BODY AS BARE LIVING ENTITY. THE FIRST POINT OF DICHOTOMY

Here, at the very outset of our detailed consideration, we are faced by one of the greatest of all difficulties. This is the point where great and fundamental contradictions can arise between the two distinct sources of our knowledge in matters that concern moral theory: between the immediate data of instinct, based upon intuition, and those which depend upon reflection within the region of the metaphysics of the supra-personal—a metaphysics which is hypothetical in a double sense.

My body lives. Ought it to live? Is there any axiom which relates to the life of my body?

It thus appears that we are here confronted by the question of questions within the region of particular Ethics and moral theory. This question will recur in each section of this book in a new form:—

Are there axioms within the region of applied ethics? That is, Are there data which, being intuited in a single instance, are intuited to be definitive?

There is an instinct which causes me to avert or to avoid harm and danger threatening my body, even when "I" am unhappy in my soul. But this instinct is no more than an innate "tendency" or "impulse". Essentially after all this impulse is no more than a desire; its note is not "it ought to be", but "I wish".

We do not know at all, then, whether my body "ought" to live or not.

Furthermore, anyone who considers these problems has at once to consider certain relations which refer him beyond the mere object "my body" and put him into contact with "my soul" as the object of ethical consideration.

For if my body "ought" not to live, then surely my soul ought to contribute to the cessation of its life, and this fact would be manifested to me as will and deed, both being a part of my consciousness. To put it in popular language: "I" would have to will the cessation of the life of my body.

The question, then, is: What ought I to will, in the ethical sense, with respect to my body as living entity? It is this that we now have to discuss.

This, then, is our first question. Two answers are possible, which depend upon our metaphysical convictions, and two answers have as a matter of historical fact been given. Thus at the very beginning of our discussion we meet that which we propose, in the course of our study, to call the *point of dichotomy*. Unfortunately it will continually recur as we proceed in our investigations.

If the realization, on earth and in matter, of an entelechy

is evil, and if it is the case that it were better if it did not take place, then my body as living entity *ought* not to be. If on the other hand this realization is part of the world-plan, then it *ought* to be. This is a fundamental question; it stands above feelings of sentimental pity. Even the body of the supporter of a family ought not to be as a living entity if (for example) its death contributed magically to the salvation of all mankind and of creatures generally.

We will now assume that the love of life was given the psycho-physical person because life on earth is part of the world-plan. This of course also applies to "my" life.

On this assumption I "ought" not to kill myself. The question thus never arises which is more just ethically—immediate and violent suicides, or self-destruction by means of starvation.

However, our ethical assertion is based upon a mere assumption; and we may say already at this place that the question whether in certain circumstances I may suffer myself to be killed voluntarily will be separately discussed at a later point.

It might here be said that one possibility has been neglected: in itself it may be morally indifferent whether my body lives or does not live, and the only question which arises may be whether I live "for" some other person. But this is not one of the questions which deal with the so-called "duties towards myself" in the strictest sense. The only question to be investigated is whether my body, taken simply as living body in itself, would be better alive or dead. The whole of this investigation is of the highest class metaphysically; and it must be allowed that it rests upon the consideration of magical possibilities.

The only possible decision is here hypothetical, and it is reached through the assumption that the love of life which has been implanted in me must have its source in some highest principle, since no other source could be possible. Its existence, then, must be conformable to this highest source. Thus we possess an instinct, but nevertheless are a little doubtful of the metaphysical value of that which it tells us. However, we have made up our minds, although the decision which we have reached is no more than hypothetical; and we must stick to our decision for everything that is to follow in the course of our theory. This much follows from our principle of the validity ef all axioms and pseudo-axioms (p. 65).

(b) MY BODY AS INSTRUMENT OF THE SOUL

The question whether my body as such ought to live has now been hypothetically answered in the affirmative; in other words, the discipline of death (as we may call it for short) has been rejected by postulate. It is only at this point that the question about the moral position of the body as an instrument of the soul has any meaning. Here, too, although we are dealing with the body, the whole problem is approached once more from the point of view of my soul and of my volition and activity as ego;

and this is done even more emphatically than at the point where the only question at issue was the life of my body.

We are not yet asking how I ought to use the body as an instrument for the execution of actions: this is a moral question which concerns my soul alone; but we are asking what I ought to will with respect to the instrument in general if I am to be a man of "good will".

I have reached the hypothetical decision that my body as living entity ought to exist, although I am well aware that there are many Indians whose answer would be in a different sense. Once this decision has been made, some further conclusions are reached about my obligations towards the body as instrument in general, provided at least that at the same time we concentrate our attention upon the empirical datum which is called the life of a psychophysical person of my species.

If I will and ought to live, then I must do so in the world with which circumstance has surrounded me, and I must live in it as an acting entity. For in man even the simplest bodily functions are, at least in part, actions which are willed or not willed. I act with my body for instrument. Even the care of the instrument itself requires the instrumentality of the instrument. It is with this that we are here concerned.

My duty towards my instrument is, then, to employ the instrument in such a way that it remains an instrument fit for use.

This follows from the assumption that "I ought to live"; for life is a component of the surrounding world.

This conclusion is also reached in another way through instinct. I have not only an impulse after life: I have also been endowed with an impulse after health, which definitely carries a note of pleasure. If, as we are assuming, it conforms with the plan of the source which is its origin, then it tells us: "Your body ought to be fit as an instrument—that is, it ought to be healthy."

It should be fit for action. The question arises, What actions? For of actions there are many.

At this point, however, we are not yet concerned with the various directions in which the body as instrument may be trained. The only demand at this point is that the body shall not be sick—that is, that one or the other part of it shall be fit to be used as instrument as occasion may demand, and that its efficiency may be increased if necessary.

B. Duties Towards My Soul

We now come to the duties towards my soul.

What ought to be the nature of my soul purely as such, or, to put it more strictly, what *must* be the nature of my soul, in order that I shall be able to describe it as good?

When we were speaking of the body we were unable to avoid completely any reference to the soul; for every act by which the body is influenced is carried out through the soul in so far as such an act can be willed at all.

Here, however, we are dealing with the soul alone. I am contemplating it from the ethical point of view: what do I wish the nature of my soul to be?

(a) MY SOUL AS ACTING ENTITY IN GENERAL

Here once more we reach those two contradictory systems of metaphysics, both of which are hypothetical and indemonstrable: once more we have reached the point of dichotomy. Either my soul ought to be without any wish, and ought not to possess that state which I experienced consciously as will or volition; it ought to be wholly meek and submissive and utterly patient. Or else my soul ought to be active and ought to be preserved in a state where it is fit for action.

The first must be the position of those who consider that life, although it ought not to be destroyed actively, is a punishment to be endured in silence and by each man for himself. The less he wills, the more quickly will a man reach the appointed end of his punishment, and the more salvation for others will he effect thereby. Thus once more indifference to everyday sympathy is a sign of the most intense participation in suffering.

The second position has on its side not only intellectual but also certain "instinctive" reasons, and hence we will decide in favour of the second: there is an impulse after action, and there is pleasure at the completed action. It is to be noted carefully that in the first instance there is merely impulse after action in general and pleasure at the completed action in general. We are not yet concerned with any further particulars.

My instinct tells me, then, that the attitude of my soul ought not to be quietistic.

This is the right place at which to establish a close relation between an understanding of phenomenology in general and psychology on the one hand, and Concrete Ethics and moral doctrine on the other. Such an understanding is to extend to all the individual propositions of moral doctrine, both those which have been and those which remain to be discussed: and this place is peculiarly fitted for such a discussion, since the danger of misunderstanding is greatest at this place.

The case is, then, that "I" have intuition of, and consciously possess, an indeterminate something: but I do not possess *myself* as acting, or even as becoming, entity. If I intuit ethically, I intuit under the form of "it ought to be", and that is all.

Hence also I do not "cause" my soul to be in a state of volition or non-volition, to be active or quietistic: I merely intuit that it *ought* to be the one or the other. Now it is an empirical rule that when I have intuited an "I ought" referring to my soul, then my soul often, but not always, afterwards conforms with that of which it has intuited that it ought to be. To this extent I may, in a certain measure, take pleasure in an ethical intuition with regard to my soul. For, metaphysically speaking, the real foundation of my soul intuits itself, at least in part, when *I* am intuiting; and thus in a certain manner this self-intuition denotes a turn towards the good in my soul. Unfortunately it denotes no more than a turn, since an intuition of the good is one faculty and a capacity for doing it another, as we knew, although perhaps the two faculties are not wholly disconnected.

I intuit, then, that my soul ought to be fit for action, and I hope that now it has the power to act.

We are here speaking only of action in general, and not of action in particular. Now I intuit that empirically there are different possibilities of particularized action; perhaps, then, it will prove possible to say a little more without necessarily entering upon particularities of action as such.

(b) MY SOUL AS CONTAINING PARTICULAR DISPOSITIONS

Souls have different dispositions with regard to the different classes of particular action, and my soul, too, has different dispositions in different degrees.

From the injunction that the soul is to be kept fit for action in general it follows immediately that it must be kept fit in a particular manner for those forms of action for which it has the strongest aptitude, provided that such dispositions have something good for aim.

The general injunction of moral doctrine must then instruct us not to allow those our faculties which are turned upon a good end to decay by disuse; provided that action has been understood to be something which ought to be. To put it more strictly, I judge of my soul

F

that it ought to be as it is, if those its dispositions which are turned upon a good end did not decay by disuse.

As an injunction this amounts to a rejection of idleness and sloth. At the same time it is an injunction which instructs us to try every means which will serve to strengthen the soul—for example, auto-suggestion.

On the other hand, the soul ought not to be active aimlessly. Every man who does work knows—and the higher the sphere in which he works the firmer is his knowledge—that he cannot do valuable work at all times; there are certain times when he experiences a kind of call: at such times he can do good work, at others the work which he does is of inferior quality.

We will here formulate our injunction in the terms, "Open the faculties of your soul at the hours when the call comes to you"; and we will add, "Pay heed to the call, but allow rest to your soul at other times". We are, of course, aware that an injunction is just a compendious manner of implying that, "It would be good if it were so".

What dispositions I am to lay open is a question which can be answered only subjectively and in the form of a confession; for here we are within the region of the exact concept of *duty* in its peculiar sense. I, and I alone, know what my soul can do and ought to do. And this, as perhaps I may say already at this point, is true of every "I". To this must be added the talent for intuition as such, which is an utterly personal matter. At this place demonstration is superfluous, and it is necessary only to add that the life of meditation is reckoned as a life of action, the foundations of which *ought* to be strengthened, where a man has a talent for it. For meditation is a different matter from quietism, which has been banned by postulate (p. 80), and it is also a different matter from asceticism (pp. 75 sqq.).

(c) THE PURITY OF MY SOUL

There is, however, yet another empirical and universally valid injunction for the soul: an injunction of which Kant was aware when he spoke of the dignity of man as the bearer of the moral law. In this section we are dealing only with the dignity of *my* soul.

In the form of my personal intuition my soul has the power of apprehending that which *ought to be*. Evidently, therefore, my soul would be good, and would be in good case, if it always intuited the good and nothing but the good, and if it passed on to "me" no particular contents which are evil. Let us call this state the purity of the soul, or else its dignity.

In the shape of an injunction, or at any rate of a wish, the moral law of the dignity of my soul may be formulated in the words, "May my soul be pure and consequently worthy of its great faculty of intuiting the good in the form of personal intuition".

In its strongest form the same injunction runs, "the soul *ought* to be holy".

The theory of the dignity of the soul is, surely, superior to metaphysical contradictions: perhaps the right place for dealing with it would have been at the general introduction to moral theory, since at bottom it is nothing other than the theory which was dealt with at that place and states that the foundation of the whole of ethics is to will one's own good will—only here the theory is fully elaborated. Kant, of course, saw all this, although he took it as applying to the dignity not only of my soul, but also to that of others. We will speak of this at a later place. Kant did not emphasize sufficiently that the idea of the dignity of the soul is something new in contrast to the supreme and purely formal demand of ethics which is expressed in the categorical imperative.

If we say that the soul "ought" to be pure—that is, that it ought to present to my conscious experience nothing but what is good—this tells us nothing at all about that in which the good is to consist in particular. This can result only from the later course of our exposition. It is this very fact which gives to the concept of dignity its universal significance.

3

DUTIES TOWARDS MY NEIGHBOUR, *QUA* INDIVIDUAL PERSON

We now leave the duties towards myself and pass over to the duties towards others. At this point the "Other" is *any* other person, so that the totality of the Others may be denoted in one word by "all". At the same time we know very well that the attitude of the self must always form the starting-point of the discussion—that is to say, that that which at another place[1] we called retrospective moral intuition must come first. At this point, however, my body and my soul have ceased to be the object of the action upon which my intuition is directed.

In all that follows the validity of the moral propositions which we have reached is presupposed, and everything accordingly depends upon the validity of the proposition, "My body ought to live and to be fit, and my soul ought to be fit and pure".

If it were better that there were no life at all, and if *ought* were consequently to be destroyed immediately or otherwise, then it would be meaningless to trouble about the particular details of the life of another (except perhaps in order to destroy it); and if it were better that there were no action, and if Auto-Quietism were most to be desired (even in the sense of supreme fellowship in suffering), then there could be no place for any action in particular.

A. PROPAGATION

The First Apology.

The most fundamental act by which I, as psycho-physical person, enter into relation with an external life is propagation, since this is the cause of a new life. Our first question, then, is whether there ought or ought not to be

[1] Cp. Driesch, *Ordnungslehre*. Second edition, 1923, p. 424.

propagation—that is to say, with respect to the empirical facts of human sexual propagation, whether the sexual act ought or ought not to be.

Now if I have assented to my own life, and have thereby admitted hypothetically that life is part of the unknown plan of the world, then I must go a step farther and give moral sanction to the sexual act as the means of propagation. So far purely hypothetical metaphysical considerations will carry us.

To these must be added an "instinctive" element. But, curiously enough, this instinctive element is ambiguous, and not unambiguous like the impulsive striving after life in general and after health and fitness.

Besides the impulse towards the sexual act there is also the feeling of modesty. None but the cynic takes pleasure in speaking of this act. The question now is, Which of these two instincts deserves greater weight in moral matters. In my opinion greater weight should be attached to the positive instinct.

The reason for this is that modesty might have an egoistic kernel: it might be based upon a false sense of dignity.

Of egoism as such we shall speak at a later place. It will be admitted that one of the forms in which it appears is self-assertion, in the sense that a man wishes himself to be the origin of as many events as possible. Now the sexual impulse is stronger than a man's self, and this is an offence to self-esteem. One wishes to be subject to none, not even to the supra-personal.

The question may be asked why there is such a thing as an impulse after self-assertion if here (and, as will be seen later, in another field as well) it is clearly in antagonism with another impulse, when admittedly the origin of everything is in the highest.

To answer this question we take up the position of our fundamental dualistic metaphysical view, and reply that the highest, when it is fettered by matter, cannot attain a pure manifestation.

There *ought* to be self-assertion within limits in so far as there ought to be any efficient action at all. But my own action may not interfere with that of others, for the action of others has its origin in the supra-personal as well as my own. This will be discussed at a later point. Further, my own action has no right to oppose itself immediately to the supra-personal.

Accordingly, although the sexual act may injure an exaggerated feeling of self-dignity, it will not injure a feeling of dignity which remains humble in the face of the highest. It is true that we are presupposing that life ought to be, although we do not know to what end. There is an impulse in me to create life; hence it ought to be so.

Of course, this argument affords a moral justification only to the normal sexual act having a normal aim.

If we leave the guidance of instinct and look for other criteria to tell us whether there ought or ought not to be propagation, then we shall discover one empirical fact which will weigh heavily against it, namely, the pangs of child-birth. If the supra-personal entity wills the propagation of life, it may be asked why it causes the realization of propagation to be accompanied in each instance, at least among the higher animals, by pain and even by danger of death. Has this fact a positive metaphysical significance, or does it follow from the fact that form is held fettered in matter?

We do not and cannot know the answer, and we will therefore refrain from judging the case.

Further considerations might lead us to the conclusion that, while there ought to be life, there ought not to be "too much". Here the dualistic world-view might give rise to something that at the first glance looks like a moral contradiction or "antinomy"—a contradiction the two sides of which must be balanced against one another in order that it shall be removed. For of course there cannot be an ultimate moral contradiction embodied in objects, since the realm of ethics is the index of one single total and supra-personal entity. In the ethical realm a contradiction can exist only for my incomplete knowledge.

If, then, there is "enough" life, the sexual impulse ought to cease. The impulse, however, does not ask after this *enough*, but continues to exist. Ought it to be satisfied? Is it right to satisfy it and at the same time to prevent propagation, which is its natural end?

Here we are faced immediately by a question which in our time has been often and gravely discussed.

In my opinion it may be possible to apologize for, but

not to justify, the sexual act where propagation is prevented. This leads us to introduce the concept of *apology* into our considerations, which implies "not good, but less not-good than its opposite". An apology for the practice which we have mentioned is possible on one definite assumption, namely, that man has certain supreme spiritual gifts, and that he ought (as we know) to develop them at those times when he receives a call. Now if the impulse hinders the free development, then he may satisfy it, even though propagation is prevented. This "ought" not to be, but it *may* be, because if it were not something higher would be harmed. It is to be hoped that physiology will succeed in discovering a means of cutting off the sexual impulse without doing harm to health or fitness of body or soul. Those who call this interference with nature should consider that so-called reason too is a part of nature, or, if this concept is taken in the narrow sense, of the empirical reality which is interconnected with nature.

The truth is that our world is a dualistic world: we are at the same time angels and beasts. The best course is to accept this fact with a smile. All that indignation can do is to hinder something higher, and that would be the greatest harm of all.

It is true that this is not enough to allow us to say that the sexual act, where propagation is not intended, is morally indifferent. There is nothing that is morally indifferent. In fact it is quite clear that it ought not to be, for to a certain extent it is contrary to "dignity". But we

stand in a dualistic world, and we shall see that there are
many occasions when we have to make our estimations of
good a matter of degree. Now it is better to leave a free
course to the realization of high gifts than to preserve
one's own dignity by denying satisfaction to an impulse.
All this, of course, is true only on the assumption that
life and effective action "ought" to be, and that abstention
is not supposed to have a magical effect. Thus by postulate
ascetic practices of any kind which would imply harm
to the power of effective activity are prohibited; but this
is not to say that the man who abstains without thereby
doing harm to himself (and this applies to every form of
abstention) is not the ideal after which to strive.

B. General Remarks relating to that which is to
FOLLOW

Egoism and Altruism

We now come to consider those duties towards another
which comprise the great bulk of the matter which is
commonly dealt with under the name of a moral theory or
system of ethics.

Here we must say in the first place that the common
concept of duty, if it is taken strictly, never occurs in an
absolutely unadulterated form. My relations to others are
always affected in part by my fellowship in the life of
others, as already defined, and, as we know, this fellowship stands side by side with duty, unless, indeed, we call

duty everything whatever of which we intuit that it ought to be. Duty in the narrower and wholly personal sense can exist only where fellowship in life is an original datum.

When I analyse my duties towards another I invariably treat him, too, as having duties—as a person who has duties towards himself. That is to say, I consider him as an ethical subject who stands to me in the relation of object. The essence of duty is to be wholly personal, and therefore his duties towards himself must remain quite indeterminate: they can have empirically universal validity only to this extent, that at most I can morally impute to another (to use Kant's expression) a faculty for preserving life and fitness. Even this restricted validity can be no more than hypothetical. He should develop his faculties, but what his faculties may be I do not know. His metaphysical convictions may even be different from mine, and in that case every trace of universal validity would vanish, even with regard to the preservation of life and of mental and bodily fitness: all that could possibly remain would be the demand that the soul shall be pure.

Thus I can speak of my duties towards another only in so far as a fellowship in life subsists between him and me; and we shall see that even of these duties only a small number is universally valid.

It is true that all this is simplified by the fact that we need not here expressly emphasize the distinction between body and soul: the other person may be treated simply as psycho-physical man (or beast). I can act immediately only upon the body of a man (if we neglect telepathic phenomena); indirectly, on the other hand, such action always in some manner affects his soul.

From all that has been said here it follows that all that part of ethics which refers to our attitude to others is clearly no more than a means to the attainment of the highest ethical end, and is never turned immediately upon this end. The others stand in the service of the highest; they do so in some form, although I do not know in what, and for this reason alone I am in a state of ethical obligation with regard to them. Thus the ethics of duty proper in the narrower sense comes much closer to the Ultimate and the Highest than do those actions which are dealt with most exhaustively in the traditional systems of ethics. On the other hand, we must not forget that an ascetic by conviction will not take any notice whatever of the "Other", in order that he shall not be distracted from his highest sympathy, which is a magical action. The convinced ascetic here stands in an immediate ethical relation to the metaphysical ultimate, and in the face of this latter everything is indifferent.

If I can undertake any actions at all with regard to the "Other" of which it is possible to predicate that they ought to be, then this means that there are actions which ought to be which have for object to bring about some state in another and not in me. At this stage it is quite indifferent what this state is. *Alter* is Latin for "Other", and such actions are called altruistic.

Latterly it has become a commonplace of popular ethics that there is no such thing as an altruistic action. It is said that every action which is approved ethically brings a note of pleasure for its subject; that the alleged altruistic action has for real motive the pleasure which it beings to the subject; and that accordingly it is egoistic. This view completely mistakes the phenomenological facts; for, after all, there are actions which have for end an ethically definitive alteration in the state of an "Other"—an end which is ethically approved and which is the simple object of these actions: they have no other motive. In most instances the ethical pleasure which they bring with them, and which, as we know (p. 29), is better called joy, is not thought about at all. This may happen, nevertheless, for example, with persons who are inclined to think much about themselves, but even with them the anticipation of the pleasure which is to come very frequently is not the motive. I think, further, that it never is the motive in what we may call energetic actions—for example, when a man jumps into a river in order to save a child. On the other hand, we surely need not trouble ourselves about those people who subscribe to charity in order that their names shall appear in the list of donations.

There are, then, altruistic actions, in spite of the fact that every ethical action brings pleasure with it.

We must now proceed to deal with these altruistic actions.

We must ask what axioms there are and what propositions follow from them, *given* the empirical state of facts and all the possible facts the existence of which the nature of the world admits.

This question is one of the most important, and at the same one of the most difficult, in the whole of ethics.

The fundamental question—and it is extremely difficult —is that which deals with the axioms or axiom. Is there anything here that is of axiomatic nature—that is, anything that is definitive and perfectly certain, and not to be improved upon? On what kind of datum could the evidence be based? Surely on nothing else than a quasi-instinctive intuition which immediately apprehends particular data. Metaphysical reflection can give us no more than a probability which can at best be looked upon as a kind of pseudo-axiom.

Let us, then, begin this investigation with a warning: granted that we had something genuinely axiomatic, or something only relatively certain, which we look upon as a pseudo-axiom, then no infringement of this may be admitted in the further course of the development of the moral theory, and no later proposition may be allowed to be in conflict with it.

But this is the very fault of which the ethical systems with which we are familiar have been guilty only too frequently in the field which we have been considering. An attempt is made to find a place within the system for desires which are anything but ethical (although we hope that the author of the system is not clearly aware of this), and in the course of this attempt principles are surrendered which had previously been asserted to be

fundamental; and it is overlooked that such a proceeding is like that of a geometrician who should waive the
theorem of Pythagoras on occasions when it suits him.

We too, of course, make a distinction between justification and apology (p. 88); and we also know that the
concept of apology is forced upon us by the dualistic
nature of the world. But this does not turn apology into
justification; and an action for which no more than an
apology can be offered is not one which plainly and
evidently proclaims that it ought to be.

My life and my spiritual and bodily efficiency and
development ought to be. But this is the case only because
these things ought in general to be.

Hence all life, including its psycho-physical efficiency
and development, ought to be promoted by me as acting
entity, and ought in no circumstances to be hindered.
(The latter injunction follows as an obvious corollary.)

This sounds as though it were the result of reflection,
derivative and not axiomatic. In fact it is actually derived
from something that is not even ultimate in itself: for
that life ought to be was not acknowledged universally, to
say the least of it.

The question now is whether after all there is not some
original intuition which is independent and is turned
immediately upon altruistic action. Perhaps there is even
one which is veritably definitive, and is more clear and
definite than that which tells us that our own efficient
life ought to *be*, being rooted immediately in the nature of
"impulses".

It seems to me that my experience presents two fundamental phenomena which quite immediately forbid me to harm "another" (even an animal) and urge me to do good to the Other. Of these the first is the pang of conscience which invariably follows the action by which the Other is harmed, and the second, the calm of conscience which invariably follows the action by which the Other is benefited. Both these phenomena exist, and the first of them exists even in the criminal, if only in the form of a strange unrest of conscience which is not due simply to fear of punishment; often it exists in a much stronger form and leads the criminal to give himself up.

At this point we reach very grave difficulties which will accompany us throughout the whole course of our investigations.

What is the position when I do good to one person by doing harm to another? In that case my action would not, of course, be something that ought to be: *that* it could be in no circumstances. But still it ought perhaps to be rather than another action, since after all we live in a dualistic universe. In that case we would have to weigh one against the other, at any rate—although we do not yet know this—in favour of certain actions which ought to be if not absolutely, at any rate relatively. At this point we may cite as examples punishment and self-defence.

Thus we are once again faced with the concept of apology.

Now, however, we must attempt to see whether there is a class of harm which is prohibited in all circumstances, even if it does good to others indirectly; and whether there are actions which do good of a fundamental kind, and are to be executed in all circumstances.

C. THE COMMANDMENT WHICH FORBIDS KILLING

The greatest harm that can be inflicted is to kill. The question now arises whether the sixth commandment, "Thou shalt not kill", ought to be allowed unrestricted validity; whether it ought to be counted a true axiom of concrete ethics.

Killing in the form of murder is an act of such a kind, that whoever can commit it without pangs of conscience is no longer considered an ethically normal person, but as suffering from moral insanity. But every normal person also experiences an exceedingly powerful feeling of repugnance when he witnesses an execution, or, at war, an act of killing. Even when an animal is slaughtered pity is caused, at least in those who are unspoilt—that is, who are not habituated. It may have been noted that nobody likes to relate his war-experiences. The good are sorry to have taken part in it; and those who are morally in the dark—we do not say the wicked—try to drown in cheers their rising disgust. And they too are not fond of talking.

It seems to me that here we have that which we are looking for, namely, pity with the being that is to lose its life by violence. As a matter of supra-personal and empirical reality we experience with irresistible strength

G

the intuition that this ought not to be, just as we experience with irresistible conviction, in geometry, and even against the evidence of our senses, the intuitive knowledge that parallel straight lines do not intersect. This intuition refers quite immediately to the object; the idea that all this might happen to me too (which would turn everything into egoism) has no place here. The reflective apprehension of the significance of this irresistible and intuitive pity comes later, just as in geometry. Instinct had already thrown an inner light upon that which, later on, reason makes clear to me.

Reflecting reason now asks why I ought not to kill, quite apart from murder.

Here it is not hard to adduce a number of reasons which follow from the considerations which we discussed in those sections which have already been dealt with in the course of this book.

The man who has been killed, for example by being executed, might have gained in dignity, or might have mended his ways, and it is this precisely which ought to be. The man who has been killed, for example at war, might have had talents of the highest kind, the development of which would have been of greater value than anything that was gained by his death for some other cause, for example, that of the preservation of the state. Our meaning will be correctly apprehended if we imagine Jesus or Goethe killed at the age of twenty. And, more generally, the other man ought not to be killed because he is essentially of the same dignity of soul as I.

But all this is beside the mark, although for some it is an argument that is not without weight. It is even more beside the mark that to be killed is painful. For nobody can tell whether the man who was killed young might not have died later of cancer, and in much greater pain; and often death through a bullet in the head is beyond doubt a happy death. What is essential is something quite different, but something that admittedly is no more than a metaphysical possibility:

I ought in principle never to kill a living being, for I do not know what death is.

Perhaps it is true, as so many religions teach, that at the hour of death the state of the soul is of eternal importance for the soul. If this is true, then it might be the case— it might be, although I am not certain that it is so—that I had inflicted an injury upon the being which I have violently killed; an injury which goes far beyond the fact that he has ceased to live and beyond the fact which I had desired to bring about: for that which I desired to bring about when I killed him was only that he should no longer be alive, or perhaps even that he should merely be defenceless—for example, that he should cease to be a fighting soldier. But I did not desire to do any harm for the time after his death, and yet perhaps this is what I have done.

But I can also do metaphysical harm to the person the development of whose talents I stop by killing him. I am not thinking here of that which we have already discussed—of the harm done to society by the killing of a gifted member. I mean this, that nobody can say that each man has not a definite task to fulfil during life, and that it is of importance for him after death to have fulfilled it. By killing him I would thus be cutting him off from this fulfilment. This consideration is somewhat similar to certain ideas which are familiar in Indian philosophy.

Here we can clearly see the peculiar position of killing among all other forms of injury: it is something quite monstrous, for it means that by my will I fling another man into the uncertain; I inflict something upon him about which I am wholly unable to judge.

There are, of course, not many men who follow the sixth commandment quite rigorously. Most of them live in India. They alone are wholly good, and with regard to this fundamental commandment their soul is pure.

Some people now proceed to make up apologies about the application of the injunction about killing. It is to apply only to man: animals it is lawful to kill if they are harmful or if it is desired to consume their dead bodies for food.

The second argument (that which relates to the killing of animals) is the most transparent self-deception. It is perfectly possible to live on plants; less than this, it is true, we cannot do in this dualistic world until chemistry has taken some further steps forward; a possible apology can exist only for the inhabitants of the polar regions. The first argument belongs to the treatment of self-defence, which still remains to be discussed.

Once the commandment not to kill has been restricted to man further apologies are brought forward, such as capital punishment, self-defence, defence of others when attacked, war, and euthanasia. These are the words with which a bad conscience seeks to justify that which in no circumstances can be justified, but can at best be apologized for: for the language of conscience is inexorable.

But perhaps there is here something for which at least an apology might be offered.

D. Where Killing is prohibited generally, what Apologies can be brought forward?

This is not the place where we can speak of war: here we are speaking only of the relation of one human being to another human being. Here, as we shall soon see, there are in fact certain apologies, and thus it might be the case that war, which is an exceedingly complex event, might be excusable in certain circumstances. This much we may admit already at this point.

Capital punishment is not to be admitted in any circumstances. There are substitutes which completely fulfil all that can be intended by a punishment, such as security, deterrent effect, and satisfaction of justice, besides leaving open the possibility of improvement which is removed by capital punishment. From the ethical point of view there can be no further discussion of this matter.

We admit an apology for self-defence and for measures taken to repel an attack upon others (such as a homicidal assault upon myself and others) even if they lead unintentionally to killing, and even if they can lead to the desired result only by means of intentional killing, but only in quite definite circumstances, namely, where the worth of the person attacked is clearly higher than that of the attacker. It is a great evil if matters are here carried to the point of killing; it ought never to be so, and instead of killing we ought merely to render the assailant harmless. But, unfortunately, there may be cases where this is impossible. In that event the murderer is in all circumstances impure after his deed, and the person who does not resist the evil is purer, or "good". But this world is a dualistic world, and where an attack against others is warded off by means of killing, especially if the defender risks his own life, it is possible to urge an apology for the act. In this case it is irrelevant to charge the defender with egoistic self-esteem, although we do not mean to assert that it is impossible for a person to estimate his own worth quite objectively. Such would be the case where a woman defends herself against a sadistic assailant.

Euthanasia has become a matter for ethical consideration only recently. If a person is suffering great pain from a malady which in the opinion of "all" doctors is incurable, the question arises whether a doctor may kill him painlessly if he expresses the wish in full consciousness. A strong man cannot have this will, but if a weak man has it, an apology may be possible if he is killed, and this brings about his euthanasia. Legislatures will of course have to exercise great care and prudence here, else an opportunity will occur for crimes of every kind. By what means this is to be effected does not concern us here.

Euthanasia can also, of course, be attained by means of suicide: an apology would be possible for it in this case. For the rest, this section has settled the question which was raised at an earlier point; are there any circumstances apart from an incurable and painful disease in which I may allow myself to be killed? If my death will serve to save another valuable life, then I may passively incur the risk of being killed. (This may happen where I save others from attacks or effect a rescue in the mountains or at sea.) The man who is ready to give up his own life in the service of that which he considers better is what is called a hero. Ethical approval has rightly been accorded to him even when that which he thought to be the better could not in fact be recognized for something which ought to be, as happens in the case of a soldier.

E. The Injunctions against inflicting Harm

The injunction against killing, for which an apology can be accepted only in certain definite circumstances, is of greater importance ethically than all other injunctions which forbid the infliction of harm. We shall therefore devote only a little space to them, prefacing our particular remarks by the more general one, that in the region of moral doctrine, in so far as it is of a negative nature, it is well in practice to cling to the injunction which tells us not to do to others what we would not wish to suffer at their hands. It is true that this proposition as such has nothing to do with ethics, but it *is* true that genuine ethical action falls under the relation which it sets up. For in the profoundest sense of the word the practice of ethics, whether active or passive, brings with it the highest happiness.

I "ought" not to inflict pain upon any living being— pain either of the body or of the soul—for pain inhibits; nor ought I to hamper it in the free development of its faculties. By free I mean that which is in conformity with its nature. When either rule is infringed it is customary to offer apologies.

It has already been mentioned that the injunction that another must not be hampered implies that pain must not be inflicted upon another. Hence it is clear that an acceptable apology may be offered for the infliction of pain where the facts are analogous to those cases in which killing might be admitted by apology, if not justified: for example, where attacks, especially attacks upon others, are warded off. It is obvious without discussion that a doctor may inflict pain in order to heal.

There remain pain inflicted for the pleasure and for corporal punishment. We need not say much about the first. It merely serves the pleasure of him who inflicts it, and this pleasure is based upon the lust for power, unless indeed it is a pathological case. Corporal punishment is to be condemned in our opinion, even for children, and even where it is not accompanied by feelings of anger or revenge, but is inflicted quite calmly. The reason why we condemn it unequivocally in these cases is that it is contrary to the dignity of man, and even of an animal. The being on whom corporal punishment is inflicted is treated simply as a body; the attempt is made to master him in a purely physical manner; he is reminded that he is matter as well as spirit. But this means that his just consciousness of dignity, and his spiritual side, is hurt. There can be no greater spiritual harm than this recalling of his lower part. We all know the pitiable, frightened look which men (and animals) wear throughout their life who were beaten when they were young. They have lost for ever the share in self-dignity which is theirs by right. (This may apply also to whole peoples who have had to endure ruthless treatment at the hands of a certain caste, for example, a military caste or a caste of conquerors. Cp. the idea of the Inferiority Complex.)

Everybody agrees to-day that liberty ought not to be restricted in that form which is called slavery. Unfortunately, the dualistic nature of the world makes it necessary that liberty must be restricted at times—as a legal punishment, or in order to control children. For, unfortunately, there must be certain safeguards and certain means of education in order that something higher shall not be hampered; and in order that this shall be achieved the means which least degrades the dignity of man is a temporary restriction of liberty—care being taken, of course, that there shall not be the least infliction of pain or scorn. This means can and ought to serve the end of causing in the person so punished a state of reflection, and hence repentance and betterment.

F. The Rule which enjoins the fostering of Talents

Up to this point our moral doctrine, which deals with the relation between myself and other living beings, has consisted entirely in prohibitions. The question now arises whether we cannot go further than this.

It has often been observed that all the ten commandments, with the exception of the fifth, are of a negative nature, and in this connection it has been remarked that moral consciousness is like the *daimonion* of Socrates—of a disapproving and not of an approving nature.

However, we do not think that this altogether meets the case. All that we can admit here is that ethical intuitions of the form of "it ought not to be" are accompanied by a stronger note of feeling (in the shape of a note of displeasure) than are intuitions having the form of "it ought to be", where the note is one of pleasure. In all probability there are metaphysical reasons for this, for the psycho-physical person is a member of the series of pure "form" which, so to speak, has entered into contact with (neutral) matter. Accordingly it does not require so much to be reminded of that which conforms to its inner nature, as of that against which it ought to be on guard because an unhappy concatenation renders it disparate with it.

On the other hand, it is precisely man, who has a full knowledge of his own nature, who knows perfectly well what he ought to do in his relations with other individual beings, and not only what he ought to refrain from doing.

It is true that here all that is particular is instinctive

only to a small degree, and is predominantly reflexive. But the fact remains that all that is instinctive is quite obviously saturated with the general, and so to speak instinctive, form of the "it ought to be".

It is true that injunctions here are exceedingly general, and that even these can exist only under the assumption which we made at the *point of dichotomy*, to the effect that it is *good* that special talents should be employed:

"Study the talents of your neighbour and assist their development to the best of your power."

Here it is true that two things remain at the mercy of my private intuition, or, if we trace the matter further back, of my intuitive capacity. These two things are, first, that which I consider a talent for the good, and secondly, that which I, having such general knowledge of mankind as I in fact possess, can apprehend of his talents. Even a good man may be a poor judge of mankind.

Accordingly care is required here, together with reticence and tact. The rule that a man should do to others as he would have them do to him holds good in moral doctrine in so far as it prohibits; but here it does not hold good as soon as we go into details. The best course, especially when we are dealing with children, is to exert an unintended and immediate influence by the example which one gives, which in this case may be called a standard. A man should try to be good himself; if he does so his influence will be for good, and that the more so, the less the influence is intended consciously. "Suggestion" by means of the example which a man gives is a factor which acts upon the soul with tremendous force.

A good example presents a man with a tangible pattern of human dignity; and if he is morally healthy he desires to achieve dignity for himself and looks upon the example in order to learn what kind of man he must be in order that he shall know that he himself is in a state of dignity.

It was of this nature that Aristotle thought the action of God upon the creatures to be when he said that God moves without being moved Himself, in the same manner as something which is the object of love—that is to say, as pattern (ὡς ἐρώμενον). Here, as in so many other places, the glance of this great philosopher went amazingly deep.

Everybody who has ever had to deal with human beings, and especially with children, knows that conscious and continual attempts at improvement by means of precepts bring about the opposite of the desired result. For every man has his just part of self-esteem which tells him that he alone is to mould himself, so that he refuses to become the subject of any other individual; the only superior whom he admits is the highest source, which is the common origin of himself and the rest, and which is manifested to him in a pure form in the shape of other individuals, and of these alone, in so far as these serve for an unconscious pattern.

It might be possible to give some details about the positive rules which ought to govern us in our relations with our neighbours; but these rules belong rather to the ethical part of sociology than to a general system

of ethics. We shall deal with them in part when we come
to investigate the formation of groups among men with
reference to the relations which *ought to* subsist among
them.

G. The Injunction to tell the Truth

We have studied the ethical relation between individuals,
and in doing so we have taken the object of action, the
"other person", more or less expressly, in his psycho-
physical double nature. In order to conclude this section
we will consider that moral relation where the two individuals are looked upon solely as spiritual beings, although
it is clear that apart from para-psychological phenomena
every action which proceeds from one individual upon
another must take place indirectly through some physical
means (speech or language).

Here only one single injunction can be applied. It is
formulated negatively as well as positively; at the same
time it is to be observed that the two formulations do
not denote exactly the same thing.

"You must speak the truth to your neighbour", "you
must not tell a lie". To begin with we will confine ourselves to the negative formulation of the injunction:
"You must not tell a lie." It is immediately obvious that
this rule is just.

For love of truth is part of the nature of spirit, and I
would be inflicting an injury on the dignity of my neighbour, and would be diverting him from his highest goal,

if I were to tell him something which to my mind expressly possessed a note of falseness.

But here, too, in certain circumstances, there may be cases where that which undoubtedly *ought* not to be still *may* be on *sufferance* in order that something that is higher and that ought to be may be in fact, it being understood that the infringement of the rule, for which an apology is thus provided, causes no harm which weighs more heavily in the negative sense than does the good which it brings about in the positive sense.

We are, in fact, discussing the emergency lie. Only pedantry can hesitate to excuse it in certain circumstances, and pedantry in this case in the last analysis is an exaggerated self-assertion of dignity. For example, if a sick man has just passed the crisis, but is still in so weak a state that any emotion would throw him back into danger, then it is permissible for me to tell him that his father, who also was gravely ill, is still alive, even if in fact he has just died.

Here love *must* carry more weight than dignity; and it will always do so. In such a case the totality must be rated at a higher worth than the perfect purity of the individual member, more especially if "I" am this member. This is true at any rate from the assumption which we made our point of departure, and which alone made possible the whole of our "earthly" moral theory: the assumption that life and action are part of the world-plan. It might be the case—as seems to be implied in certain ascetic systems—that truthfulness at all costs has an effect of magic salvation; if that were so, the case would be altered, and it would be right, in order to avoid the emergency lie, that the sick man's relapse and death should be brought about from a "highest" kind of pity. It is well at times to recall the hypothetical nature of the whole of our moral theory.

We will now briefly touch upon the positive form of the rule which we have been discussing, which is, speak the truth to your neighbour.

The emphasis here lies upon the "speak": I am to speak out the truth, if I have it in me: that is, I must not conceal it.

A spoken truth redounds to the advantage of another, or at any rate it can do so, and it is my duty to do my utmost in this direction.

It is true that here too there are exceptions, and the whole of social life is full of them. Practically everybody thinks himself, at least in some respects, the better of his neighbour, and often enough in his heart of hearts he thinks him a rather poor if not a ridiculous person.

In such a case he may spare his dignity by observing silence, quite apart from the fact that he needs must be aware that so high an estimation of his own worth demands very careful examination, to say the least of it. This is the place of all that which is called tact. Without it the whole of social life would be quarrel and irritation without end: and that would hamper the development of talents.

But, if after a conscientious examination, a man is convinced that he possesses a truth which would tend to promote the good, then he must speak it out without regard to any harm which may result to his person. This applies chiefly to the relation between friends and to that between the individual and the community, for example, in political questions.

"Moral courage" is an absolute postulate.

H. PROPERTY. WHEN IS IT JUSTIFIED?

My neighbour not only *is* something definite, but also *has* something definite, namely, that which is commonly called property. This he possesses. He may possess clothes, books, houses, cattle, plants, mines, fields, gardens, money, and many other things. What *ought* to be my moral attitude towards his property, and his to mine? *Ought* there to be any property at all in the hands of the individual? If not, there could be no moral impediment to hinder me from making use of any of the objects which my neighbour possesses for my own ends, for they all are no more than means to an end, even if the end is only pleasure; and he could similarly use my property.

Among all the things which may become a man's property there is one which differs radically from the rest, and that is money. It is a "means" in a perfectly general and indefinite manner, unless indeed it is part of a numismatic collection. At this point we will not speak of money.

If now I consider the possession of property in general, I intuit that every individual (which includes myself) *ought* at any rate to possess that which he has earned by the labour whether of his mind or of his body. (Such possession may also take the form of wages.) For each man *ought* to exercise a function, or to work—that is, he ought consciously to effect modifications in the empirical world in the service of mankind. This (hypothetical) assumption of course governs the whole of this section. Thus also the individual ought to own as his property what he has earned by his labour, and it ought to be his to dispose of at his will—to give away or to leave to his heirs. Thus property which has been given or willed away, and which had originally been earned by labour, is what we may briefly call *justly owned property*.

The case is wholly different with property which was not earned by labour, or given or left to a man after having been so earned by another. Such property he may simply have discovered, or he may have caused it to be created for himself by the labour of others, to whom he gave, with their consent, a part of his own property, or that other means of exchange which at first we did not take into consideration, namely money.

No ethical objection can be raised against the property which was created by the labour of others, provided that this labour was given by free consent to the employer, and received the wages which had been agreed upon out of the employer's stock of property, provided, further, that in the sense which we have just defined he is justified in the possession of this stock. Of course, no advantage must be taken of the necessity of the labourer who must receive

H

adequate wage. This remains to be spoken of at a later point.

The question then remains whether the possession of property which has been discovered ready at hand is "justified". This is a necessary condition in order that the property which has been created for a man by the labour of others shall be justifiably his in all possible circumstances.

Discovered property may also be called property by seizure. To this class belongs water, land, coal, ores, and other commodities when first they become the property of a man—for example, one who has emigrated into a virgin region. Coal which has unexpectedly been found under a field may also be reckoned under this class. Now it is quite certain that property which has been acquired by seizure cannot be traced back to any past labour of its owner or to justified gift or to inheritance. But up to this point these three have been looked upon as the only sources which can justify possession, so that it is doubtful, to say the least, whether discovered property, or property which is derived through such a source in any manner, may justifiably pass into the possession of the individual.

In my own opinion mineral wealth, in the widest sense of the term, *ought* not to become personal property. It is obvious that the earth, and all that exists in it or upon it in an untouched form, exists for all. The world is of such a nature that all are born into it equally and are dependent upon it for their primitive life.

Mineral wealth is a means, and as such ought to belong

to all. It ought to be lent to individuals for a term, in order that these shall exercise their energy upon it, on condition that the person who exercises his energy in the form of labour is bound to contribute to the community a part of the yield of his labour, unless, indeed, this yield is sufficient only to provide him and his dependants with a livelihood.

Land in itself must here be treated separately from other wealth of the earth. Like water and air, coal and ores ought to belong to the community and the community alone, which appoints certain persons as officials for their exploitation. Land and the water which happens to be upon it may be lent out to individuals as semi-property for their free disposal for the term of their lives or of their labouring efficiency, on the understanding that they make use of that which is lent them in order to exert their labour upon it. A certain piece of land might perhaps be given them in fairness for their recreation.

For anybody who wants to, it should be possible to borrow land from the community. He requires land for his home in any case; but he has also the right to have it for use as a garden in dimensions which remain to be settled by arrangement.

It goes without saying that property in land cannot pass by gift or inheritance, since the land itself is only lent. It might, however, be arguable that it ought to be granted for a number of generations; and here, except in the case of home and garden, the grant would be extinguished if the heirs failed to exploit the land.

To money as property we gave the name of universal means, for it can have its origin in any given form of possession, and can be changed into any given form of property. This change is justified in so far as the possession in question is justified. It is obvious that justified possession of property can have no other origin than justified original possession, and no money except such as is justly owned can be given or willed away. Money which has its origin in property that has been lent must be surrendered to the lender in part (namely, in so far as it is not the product of labour), that is, to the community as a totality—at least if we take up the standpoint of this section, where we have not yet reached the concept of the State.

Loans of money between individuals against the payment of interest has of course met with very different judgments in the course of history. Originally it was morally condemned by the Christian Church.

If we make it our principle that no property is justified except such as ultimately is the product of labour, even though it has been obtained by gift or inheritance, then interest is indeed something that ought not to be, since it means the acquisition of property without work. A powerful excuse for the practice of taking interest exists in the fact that the borrower expressly agrees to pay the interest. The practice of lending against interest can be admitted even more unreservedly if the capacity for work of the borrower is enhanced by the money which has been lent him against interest, so that he earns more than he would be able to earn without the borrowed money, even after the interest has been allowed for. In the modern economic structure of the world this is universally the case. But even here we have no more than an apology, and it *ought* to be the practice for a man who has more than he needs to lend to a capable person that which he requires in order to give full play to his capacities; and he ought to do so without any expectation of receiving back the loan in better times, although this will be the case if the borrower is a person of decent disposition.

If the community granted full powers to work to each individual in accordance with his faculties, and took care of those who are incapable of work, then the lending of money against interest would become superfluous, and would therefore have to be condemned unequivocally.

4

DUTIES TOWARDS GROUPS

So far we have used the expression "the community" to denote mankind. Empirically mankind is divided into groups, the most important of which are called family, people (nation), and state.

We have not much to say ethically about the family. It follows immediately from the highest principles that men are responsible for the bodily and ethical welfare of beings the cause of whose empirical existence they themselves are: and in practice this principle is followed with very few exceptions. Rather a warning might be in place lest men improperly prefer their own children and those of relatives to other human beings.

The family is founded upon propagation. Consequently the first question which arises (an extremely grave question) is, what ought and what ought not to be the rules governing propagation, without regard to the element of sex as such, which has been dealt with already.

A. MARRIAGE

Man has a dignity of his own, and this dignity, as we know, may be in conflict with the sexual impulse, a conflict which is an illusion when it is directed against the sexual impulse in general, but may be quite justified in certain special circumstances. In the second case the rule which is to govern propagation must be that where there is a genuine conflict between impulse and dignity, the latter should prevail. Man is a beast, but he is a human beast —that is, a beast having knowledge: *animal rationale*.

We know that the sexual impulse ought, within certain limits, to serve propagation and not mere lust; on the other hand, an apology may be offered for it where propagation is not intended and it is indulged in order to stimulate the unhampered development of faculties.

Human dignity is best satisfied by the community if sexual intercourse does not take place between any given couples at choice, but between partners whose duties towards one another are laid down in binding agreements. (At this point we are not taking the State in its proper sense into consideration.) For this is the only arrangement which adds to the community of bodies that community of souls which is called friendship and does justice to the spiritual side of man.

The sexual partnerships which are governed by agreements which are binding upon the partners are called marriages. Marriage, accordingly, *ought* to be.

Marriage may be monogamous or polygamous, and there are three varieties of the latter kind. One man may have many wives, or many men may have one wife, or many men may have many wives: the partners are imagined as remaining the same, as is implicit in the idea of marriage.

The physiology of propagation contains within it the reason why the arrangement by which many men have one wife must be condemned, since more than the rest it is contrary to human dignity. The reason is that a pregnant woman cannot for the space of a year be rendered pregnant again. The next arrangement to be rejected is that by which there would be many partners on each side, for this would do a hurt to friendship in its highest form: and friendship precisely *ought* to be.

Thus there only remain to be discussed monogamous marriage and what is known as polygamous marriage in the usual sense—one man and many wives. Roughly speaking we may say that the West has elected monogamy, and the East polygamy.

There are physiological reasons in favour of the latter form, but in spite of this monogamy is ethically the higher form, for it alone provides a maximum control of the impulse towards propagation and at the same time best fosters friendship. But it must be freely admitted that a person who is too weak to confine himself to monogamy would do better morally to take more than one wife than to break faith by having free intercourse with other women. For the latter course constitutes a lie for which there is no excuse, and is the greatest hurt to dignity.

It should be possible to dissolve a monogamous marriage without difficulty so long as there are no children. If this is not the case the position may in certain circumstances be so complex that a discussion of it would take us beyond general ethical theory.

B. BIRTH-CONTROL

We now reach a problem which has proved of particular interest in our times: the question whether the number of births ought to be controlled. Here the question is simply "whether" and not "how". We have already dealt with this question (p. 87), and all that need be said at this point will be a slight elaboration of our former remarks. It may be said, then, that of all the means for controlling births there is one only to which no ethical objection whatever can be raised, and that is self-restraint. Next to this comes free regulation of the sexual impulse with which perhaps a future physiology will supply us. After these come contraceptives, and for these too an apology may be offered.

The next question is whether there *ought* to be any birth-control at all in certain circumstances. The answer is undoubtedly in the affirmative, and will be so even more emphatically in the future, although this future may be somewhat distant. This follows from two facts: from the progress of hygienic science, and from the finite nature of the surface of the world. There will be a time when, to put it quite roughly, there will simply not be room enough for men if they multiply without restriction, and if at the same time infant mortality has approximated to zero. In that case the community, not the state, for we do not yet know that concept, will have to regulate the propagation of the individual, for otherwise survival, and still more the development of talents, will be impossible. Even in our times the question has become acute in certain regions. It is true that frontiers may be abolished, so that men will be free to settle as they please in the future: but the fact remains that the surface of the earth is finite even so. To this consideration no objections can be offered, and least of all can ethical approval be accorded to that which is urged as a consideration of state, namely, that the individual state requires numerous citizens in order that it shall be able to enforce its will.

This will become clear at a later stage. In general we are unfortunately forced to admit that birth-control is urgently demanded by the present state of the world, and will be even more urgently demanded in the future. It *ought* not of course to be, but that which will come about without it ought to be still less; this is the apology for it. It is better that the unborn be destroyed than that those who are born kill one another consciously later.

Here reason, which at the same time is morality, must be supreme.

It is to be hoped that in time we shall find birth-control by worth, by the side of numerical birth-control. The possibility has already been discussed in North America. At the moment perhaps it has a fantastic sound; nevertheless it is far from unreasonable to hope that it may some time prove possible to foretell and to encourage valuable births.

It is a different question whether at some future time it may be possible to recognize at an early stage particularly valuable individuals among those who are born—those who are destined to become men of talent or genius. Perhaps it might be possible to bring this about by means of the observations of reactions, which, although apparently quite beside the mark, are in fact in a fixed state of correlation with great gifts. If this were possible a special education might be accorded to these privileged creatures, and future leaders might consciously be reared. This is not really the place for this question; however, we may briefly touch upon it here. To-day this question may appear utopian, but perhaps it will not appear so for long. Much we cannot say about it, but we express the opinion that ethical approval ought to be given to qualitative selection of births and to special education for those who have early been recognized to possess particular talents.

C. The Nations

Nations are groups of men having a common destiny. We intentionally prefer this very vague word to one more definite. Here language very frequently is the deciding factor, although not invariably, for the Swiss possess three languages and nevertheless feel themselves to be one nation, and the Scots speak English and yet are far from considering themselves to be Englishmen, although they do feel themselves to be Britons. (It is true that they do not feel any enmity towards Englishmen.) Among Mohammedans and Hindoos it is religion, of course, which is the fundamental cause of unity.

Nations are something given in the same way in which species are given, although the genuine biological element of "race" is not so significant for them. All living nations are a mixture of "races" of the second degree, of Teutons, Celts, Latins, Slavs, quite apart from the mingling of the original races. The most that we can say is that certain racial peculiarities predominate in certain parts of the nation. But often there are great racial differences within a single people, which feels itself to be such, while there are great similarities between parts of different nations.

In a perfectly general and indefinite sense the question may be asked whether there *ought* to be lions, horses, rattlesnakes, or bees; and similarly the question whether it would be better or not that there should be Germans, Japanese, and Frenchmen (that is, whether **they** *ought* or *ought not* to be) has not really any meaning in view of our uncertainty about metaphysical ultimates. (The peoples mentioned above are mixed races, and were intentionally selected as such.)

When human communities of the highest class act, they do so in the form of the state. Consequently ethical theory has to concern itself with the state alone when it has to deal with major groups of men.

D. THE STATE

For Ethics the state is a community of men who are consciously united in order to ward off that which ought not to be, and in order to promote that which ought to be. It is founded upon certain rules which are binding upon its members; these are called the law; it is enforced by means of punishment.

It goes without saying that law ought, for the ethical student, to have ethical intuition for foundation even if in practice it is supported by force, and is immediately for the citizen a compulsion and no ethical obligation.[1] As a matter of historical fact it has always been the case that laws which originally were merely decrees dictated by the force of brutal conquerors or usurpers attained in course of time a moral quality—a symptom of the harmony of the world.

There *ought* to be but one state, for mankind is one.

[1] Some excellent observations on this matter and that which is treated immediately below will be found in Laun's *Recht und Sittlichkeit*, 1925.

But states have their origins in history, and their origins from the beginning were not what they ought to be, for they arose through the main force of individual men or groups; consequently there is empirically a plurality of states. It should be the aim of every man to make one state of the many states, for a great moral danger is contained, as will appear, in the plurality of states. Where there are many states, there everything is not yet in order. The state strives to be the expression of order among mankind, and it is thus part of the essence of the state that it shall exist in the singular. Those who argue otherwise miss the essence of the state, and are empiricists.

It would be best for *the* state, and even for any empirical state, if it could transcend itself, in conformity with its own concept, and if *an-archy*, that is, the negation of Constitution, could be its constitution; it being the case that the state needed no constitution. But this assumes that men by nature never act otherwise than well, and this unfortunately is not the case. In spite of this it is the duty of all men to make it the aim of their endeavour that there shall be one state only, and that the state, as a conscious legal institution, shall become superfluous: the ultimate end of the state is, that the state shall be transcended.

In fact, however, there is not one single state, and still less can there be any justified self-transcendance of the state. We must therefore rest content with the existence of a multiplicity of states, and must investigate what

ought to be their nature. Here we must never lose sight
of the supreme guiding rule, which is that the highest
moral end of all actions which aim at human community
shall be the removal of the state because it has become
superfluous, and the next highest the union of all states
in one state, which would still, however, be a genuine
state based upon law.

(a) THE INTERNAL FUNCTIONS OF THE STATE

(a) *General Remarks*

To begin with, we investigate the empirical individual
state as such—that is, we investigate it internally, asking
what it ought and what it ought not to be.

It must not be forgotten here or elsewhere that the
state is never anything more than a means to a supreme
moral end: it is never an end in itself. Thus the rule that
the state is to be promoted such as it is applies only in so
far as it is good as a moral structure, or in so far as it is
good. If it is not as it ought to be, then it has to be
improved. And, further, obedience can be accorded to the
laws which run in the state only in so far as they are good:
it is the absolute duty of the individual not to obey the
laws of the state without regard to punishment, if his
conscience tells him that they are not moral.

Conscience comes before obedience. It goes without
saying that this applies only to a wholly conscientious
conscience, and nothing is farther from our intention

than to recommend a lukewarm attitude towards the laws of a civilized state. But the fact still unfortunately remains that conflicts may arise, especially where the law gives positive injunctions: where it prohibits, this is less likely to happen. If such a conflict does arise, then it is true that the inner voice of conscience rather than the behests of men commands obedience.

The question now is, When are laws good? That is, when do they genuinely command obedience?

They certainly do not command it when they demand of the citizen something that is incompatible with the elementary rules of ethics, as when they demand in certain circumstances that he shall kill a man or rob him of the property which is his by right, or shall lie to him, or the like.

These words express once and for all the fundamental rule governing the relation between private ethics and state ethics. It follows immediately from our proposition about the inviolability of the ethical axioms (p. 65). If there is a conflict between these two ethical systems, then in moral theory the precedence belongs in all conceivable cases to obedience to the dictates of private ethics, which come to us through conscience. It still remains to be seen whether there is here any place for apologies; whether another course might be adopted by permission. It is certain that in the deepest sense there can be a plurality of moral codes no more than there can be a plurality of Euclidean geometries.

(β) Penal Codes

The totality of the laws by means of which the state seeks to hinder evil are called the penal code.

As a rule the penal codes of states are nowadays unobjectionable, so that they may justly command our obedience. Fortunately they do not much concern the average man, which may be entered on the credit side of the "optimistic" doctrines of the nature of man. They exist for abnormally "weak" men.

It is true, of course, that individual penalties inflicted by a criminal code may be objectionable, as we have already stated in connection with capital punishment. (Fortunately it is superfluous in these days to speak about corporal punishment as a penalty inflicted by the state, and about torture as a means of inquiry; and we will not at this point speak of the "good old times", which in truth were quite horrible times in many respects.)

Further, the provisions of a penal code may become dangerous when they relate to the self-protection of the state as such. For the state often oversteps the mark and acts as though it were a person in itself, forgetting that it never exists for its own sake, but solely for the sake of morality. We shall not discuss this fully until we come to consider from the ethical point of view the relation of the individual state to other individual states.

At this point we confine ourselves to stigmatizing any penalties which are threatened in order to restrict freedom of speech. These are contrary to the dignity of man and have no binding force. A penalty may be inflicted only where those who are of a different mind are insulted during a free exchange of opinions upon some question.

(γ) *Social Questions*

The aim of the law is not only to prevent evil, but also to promote the good, and accordingly it will manifest itself in practice; on the one hand in the shape of social legislation and on the other in the shape of rules governing culture.

Here a minimum of legislation is better than an excess, and a Socialism based upon free consent having an ethical foundation is better than State Socialism. (Such Socialism by consent is at this day to be found realized only in the United States, promoted in part by the competition between various private undertakings.) The ideal is always to have minimum of state regulation. For the state is based upon force and compulsion, and as such it has as its own supreme aim to become superfluous, an aim which is to be realized by means of education. Accordingly, that state is the best which is least noticeable.

Social legislation is directed in the main against what is called exploitation. That is, rules are made for those individuals who have become powerful through wealth, prescribing to them to what extent and at what wages they may allow others to labour for them (cf. p. 113), what damages they are liable to pay for accidental injuries, and so forth. It is true that the sphere of activities of

I

certain individuals is here restricted, but that of far more numerous individuals is extended; and accordingly social legislation at least at the present day *ought* to exist in a very full measure. From another point of view this part of social legislation might be counted a part of *prohibitive* law.

The law has a right to demand that every man shall do work of some kind, at least for a certain part of his term of life: this has its foundation in the very principles of ethics. For the world is such that work is a necessity, although in the Christian world-view this fact may be looked upon as a metaphysical punishment.

We have already spoken at another place, where it was more relevant, about those things which must be the property of the community, that is, of the state, and which must not be private property, like deposits of coal and ore, and, with certain reservations, land (p. 113).

We do not here enter upon the fundamental question of economic science—what is in principle the relation between work and wages, what is hence the value of work, and how this value is to be measured. The ethical element here consists solely in the realization that there is here a fundamental problem.

(δ) *Education. Schools*

It is the duty of the state to place at the disposal of its citizens educational establishments of every kind and without charge. It must be on its guard against any kind of pedantry with regard to admission to the higher ones among these: students will abstain of themselves from frequenting them if they do not understand what is being taught.

A certain degree of education must be compulsory, and it is right that it should be so in spite of the restriction to the freedom of the individual which goes with it. For a certain amount of compulsory education not only promotes the good of the state, but also the innermost nature of the individual, who, however, at the early period of his life with which alone we are dealing here is not competent to judge about this. In the deepest sense the compulsion of which we are here speaking *ought* not to exist, but it *may* exist permissively, for man is by nature lazy and slothful.[1]

All that may be called systematic education—we expressly come to approach this matter now—is a matter of volition. Like every other kind of volition it has two components, and these are questions which demand a solution—what is it that is willed, and how is it to be executed? Thus wherever there is volition there is also end and means, and the means can be applied proportionally to the knowledge we possess about the means available. Thus the power to execute anything that is willed is dependent upon knowledge of the laws which govern reality: for this execution is an action—that is to

[1] Some compulsion may be exerted with regard to the acceptance of offices of state, and as a matter of historical fact has at times been exerted. Those whom their fellow-citizens hold fit to assume public office *ought* not in ordinary circumstances to be allowed to refuse the office. Here again it may be possible to advance an apology for that which is of the nature of a compulsion and as such demands apology.

say, it is the realization of an event, and every action is based upon knowledge.

The educator is a willing entity, and as such he must measure his aims by an ethical standard. It ought to be his aim to produce a moral frame of mind, or at any rate an approximation to it. Then alone his aim is *good*. Those laws of reality which he must know and apply are laws of the life of the soul, and especially of the soul of the child. It follows that if his activity is to be fruitful he must have a very thorough knowledge of psychology.[1] Education from the ethical point of view is human mechanics, and without psychology it is an impossibility, as much as would be practical engineering without physics.

These general rules apply to all that is to follow.

In the first place the function of the school is to teach understanding—that is, to implant knowledge. It is true that it has also for function to strengthen the will and to form character, as the current expressions have it, but in the first instance the means to this end must be instruction— that is, reasons must be advanced. The pupil must intuit that in view of certain empirical facts or patterns it is *good* that his character should form itself in a certain manner. Instruction must be conscientious. There must be no place in the teaching of a school for authority or

[1] A knowledge of the official psychology of textbooks does not suffice: a knowledge of the psychology of the subconscious is required as well. Many fear-complexes are caused by the rash infliction of punishments, and many inferiority complexes by the rash assignment of marks in school examinations. Few are those who know that measured praise is a far more powerful lever towards proficiency and even towards self-criticism than punishment and fault-finding.

dogma, especially with regard to religion and politics. If the teacher does not know the meaning of good and bad he must freely admit it to the pupil, and that as early as possible.

There must be no contradictions between the principles which are taught. Children must not be taught in the scripture lesson to love their neighbour, and in the history lesson that in certain circumstances he may be shot dead if he belongs to a different people.

Besides instruction there is another means by which character and will may be strengthened, as Coué has taught in a scientific manner, namely, Suggestion or Auto-suggestion consciously controlled. I believe that this form of education, which makes men better through their unconscious, is destined to play a great part in the future.

Here we would deprecate any such empty phrases as that it is unworthy of the dignity of man to strengthen his character by any means save his own conscious strength of will. For we know to-day that it is the very essence of the psycho-physical nature of man to preclude the possibility that this attempt should succeed. There is no indignity, but only humility, in taking man as he is according to his essence, least of all if his innermost essence is a source of the good.

We are not here blind to the great dangers which attend the use of suggestion as a means in education. It will always have to be subject to criticism and to legislation; and in schools it will have to be confined to matters which are ethically quite certain and fundamental. The people as a whole will have to determine its limits. At all times common sense will have to go hand in hand with it. To put it briefly, the practice of auto-suggestion will always have to be willed consciously. I even go so far as to think that a child that has passed beyond earliest youth ought to have an express knowledge of the nature of the suggestive process, and ought to know that it is being subjected to it, and ought itself to will this subjection. This alone will prevent violence being done to souls.

There must be no restriction upon ethical teaching. A teacher when teaching history may even speak against the existing constitution, although he must avoid sarcasms and insults, and must tell his pupils that the questions under discussion are extremely difficult and complex, and that his own opinion, to the best of his conscience, is other than that of those men who, also consulting only their conscience, became the authors of the constitution which is in force. Grave faults are frequently committed in this matter by the parties of reaction, especially when there has been a sudden constitutional change. Thus, for example, the children of a people the constitution of which expressly aims at international peace may be instructed to hate other peoples or may be led to despise the constitution; or again, the poetry which is read, or the history which is taught, may be selected in such a way as to inculcate lessons which are ethically dangerous. This may be called undisciplined suggestion.

Serious objections may here also be urged against the

so-called classical education, or at any rate against its commonest-taught variety. Here the narrowest kind of Jingoism is cultivated. The pupil is generally told not a word about the great and world-embracing doctrines of the Stoa and of Neo-platonism, while the Persians, in spite of their lofty ethics, are treated as "Barbarians".

Those teachers who are guilty of the errors which we have described above generally commit them while practising "undisciplined" suggestion. It may be that often they practise it unconsciously. Their own doctrine is mostly based upon mere feelings and is a wholly personal view, and accordingly, in order to impose it, they have recourse to pathos, imprecations, and the like. It is precisely this undisciplined suggestion which is not to be tolerated for a moment. The teacher has the right to practise no other suggestion save that which is sanctioned by law, and his only object should be a child that has passed earliest youth and has expressly consented.

A good teacher will effect most when he acts as an example; and the stricter a master he is towards himself—in every respect—the greater will be his influence.

This much must suffice for the moral foundations of legislation in general. To conclude, we will give a general warning. No laws should be set up, and only advice ought to be given, where the frailty of human nature would cause them to be transgressed in any case. Examples of the evil effect of such laws can be found not in Germany alone. Men should never become slack and indifferent in their feelings towards the law.

(b) THE CONSTITUTION

We now come to ask who *ought* to make the laws in the state, and who *ought* to supervise their observance.

The answer to the first question is short: Every person who is mentally normal, has reached a certain age, and has attained a degree of education which will allow him to understand the question at issue.

In the narrowest sense of the word, of course, not "every person" can make and supervise any law he may choose. The problems are too numerous and too complicated to allow this. For these ends experts must be appointed. Apart from other reasons, which will soon be discussed, the number of the citizens of a state makes it impossible that "everyone" should have his voice in the matter. Accordingly, in order that the will of the state shall be executed, certain citizens who appear peculiarly fit for this post are appointed by election: these we may call officials in the widest sense of the term. To them great powers must deliberately be given. These men in turn elect, either by co-option or by the appointment of other suitable persons, special bodies who have for their peculiar function the safeguarding of the law. They also determine who is to guide their deliberations, and with them the state.

This *ought* to be the position if there is to be any state at all: and a state there must be. In principle every man must be an elector, and must be eligible for every office.

This kind of constitution is generally described as that

of a democratic republic; at any rate, we will give it that name. It is the only kind of constitution which is morally compatible with the concept of the dignity of man.

It is true that our concept of the democratic republic admits of the greatest variety of particular forms; this follows from our definition, which we intentionally made very vague, only excluding once and for all privileges of birth and property. The rules which guide us here are the following: the best ought to be directors of the state, both making the laws and supervising them. That is the common saying. And it is certain that they ought to be this, an aristocracy in the literal meaning of the word. But how are these best to be found? The fact that certain people think themselves to be such proves nothing, and the fact that their ancestors at one time were perhaps of this number is no more convincing. It is only when all give their opinion that there is any probability that the best will be found. Thus in order that aristocracy shall be reached, democracy is after all the least uncertain means. In some cases a professional grouping may be applicable, but even this must be applied in a democratic manner.

Everybody, then, except for the restrictions which we have mentioned, must have a vote. If he had not, he would be under no moral obligation to obey the laws— even the good laws. A man can bind only himself, and cannot be bound by others. It is only in democracy that the individual is a *member* and not an *object* in the state. This fact is of great significance ethically, but, so far as I am aware, it has never been clearly stated: it is only the citizen, but not the subject, who has duties towards the state.

A universal vote does not, however, of itself imply equality of votes. Here, at any rate in the discussion of technical questions, an allowance should be made for the degree of talent and of education, but for no other factors beside these. The intelligence tests of Binet and of the Americans have shown clearly how great are the differences in talent between the individuals of a single people. Not to make an allowance for this fact would be cultural suicide. To this must be added the degree of education, which does not vary with the intelligence of the individual alone. Probably it can best be measured by what may be called evidence of merit.

Each citizen, then, should have his vote. There should be additional votes for those who have special talents or have given evidence of particular fitness.

Psychological tests (and not examinations) should be used in order to determine in early youth those who have particular talents, and these should then be educated in separate schools. These are urgently needed. These persons will in practice turn towards the higher professions, and it will be unnecessary to graduate votes in order to induce them to do so.

Peculiar merit is shown up in the course of a lifetime. It can exist in every occupation, and is independent of talent, and accordingly the additional votes allotted for merit should be independent of additional votes allotted for talent. The former, however, will have to attach to a certain age. Thus a master cobbler, foreman, or head of a hospital would be allotted more votes on the grounds of merit than a cobbler's apprentice, common workman, or medical student.

Additional votes allotted for merit, and additional votes allotted for talents, should be reckoned separately, and could be added together. In this way the proved head of a hospital and the talented medical student might be allotted equal additional votes, while still obtaining fewer votes than a man having both exceptional merit and talents.

It should once more be carefully noted at this point that we allow inequality between men to play a part here only in so far as it is given naturally. Money and birth must not be allowed to carry any weight. If high birth shows itself in inherited qualities it does of course carry weight, but only in so far as the man who inherits the qualities in question has special talents or has shown peculiar merit.

This alone is true democracy. All men are reckoned equal as men. All have an equal right to confer (by means of their vote) the highest offices in the state, or to receive them (if votes are cast in that sense). But each man, being what he is, is different from every other man by nature; and this difference expressly introduces differences of degree into his active political rights; his passive rights result automatically.

Privileges exist, then, only in so far as they are, in the

last analysis, the gift of nature, and in so far as the reason for conferring them has been determined objectively—that is, by actual demonstration of higher talents or merit.

The details of any system of voting and of the appointment of officials must be left to specializing ethical theories. Here we merely say that the first election should simply have for object the appointment of an electoral body: here alone each elector is in a position to be really acquainted with the elected candidates. Or the members of this body might elect an electoral body of the second degree, leaving it to this to elect the delegates; or finally it might elect a third-degree electoral body.

Officials in the real sense must be elected in part, although not of course by the whole of the community; in part they should be appointed. Once elected, they ought to have considerable powers; among them should be the power to make certain appointments. This alone will give continuity to the state. Probably a later test of fitness for office will be necessary, perhaps through the instrumentality of a board of "censors".

We have not even hypothetically considered monarchy and "aristocratic oligarchy" as political forms; for these can possess no other honest moral foundation than a certain mystical theory of the state, a theory which in manner is theocratic. Intellectually we absolutely reject this theory. Compared with this all other objections to monarchy are of no great importance—as, for example, that it is possible that the line may deteriorate, and that the monarch might engage in friendships and enmities which may be of danger to the state. But we are not here interested in particular persons; we are concerned solely with the principle. The monarchies which are still in existence are the survivals of a mentality which no reasonable person possesses nowadays. The monarchs rule states which at bottom are democratic republics in which they are preserved as figure-heads: and the monarchs themselves are far from believing that either they or their families rule by divine right, and generally behave with extreme moderation. To this state of affairs it is not necessary to object, so long as the monarch does not forcibly pass beyond or destroy the limits of his symbolical meaning. To create a new monarchy would be wholly preposterous, and would place the monarch in a position in which, from general grounds of humanity, one would feel sorry for him. Such an innovation might even be called dishonest, for it is part of the essence of an ethical monarchy that it exists by divine right and that the monarch is a "son of heaven". The concept of a monarch makes him superhuman, and this concept is lost to us.

It goes without saying that a dictatorship acquired by force cannot be taken as an ethically acceptable political form. It is a matter of brute-force, whether its origin was on the left or the right. Those who wax enthusiastic over it probably have either themselves in mind as a potential dictator or at least one of their friends. A dictator elected by the people for a term of years is, of course, quite a different matter. Morally he is acceptable. It is true that great caution will have to be exercised in order to prevent violation of rights: at the least a very large majority and an annual reinstatement will be essential. But if these conditions are fulfilled, a dictator of true ethical bent may prove a blessing for all and not for his people alone; indeed, ethics require that he shall be a blessing for all, as will appear clearly at a later point.

Constitutions may pass out of date. In that case they must be reformed, and the question arises in what forms this is ethically permissible.

It is obvious that they may be changed in the ordinary course of legislation. But it may be that no legislative method exists which is open to the votes of the community, as happens when there is a group of powerful rulers whose domination is felt to be harmful by the majority; and in that event the position of affairs unfortunately is different. A beginning must be made with attempts to persuade. But as a rule they will not prove efficacious, for generally the rulers are not as they *ought* to be. There then remains the method of force—revolution, which morally most assuredly ought not to be, but is permissible in cases of gross misgovernment. The means by which it operates must be as mild and as unvengeful as possible, and as far as possible slaughter of the domestic enemy is to be avoided so long as he himself refrains from killing. Only when he does kill does self-defence arise, and only then can a defence be offered for killing. So far as I can see, the German revolution was the only one in history which renounced official killing—that is, executions ordered by the new organs set up by the people. Hence it was the

least immoral of all revolutions. In favour of the super-
seded authorities it must be said that they too refrained
from killing, which would have inflamed a civil war.[1]

(c) THE STATE IN ITS RELATION TO OTHER STATES

We now come to discuss the relation of the individual
empirical states to each other, which in turn leads us to
the moral theory of politics in the proper sense.

Let us begin by once more stating with the fullest
emphasis the supreme principle of moral theory, which is
that a rule which has been made in the lower stages of
moral theory may on no account be infringed in the
higher. Those who allow state morals to run counter to
private morals act (as it is worth while to repeat once
again) like a geometrician who infringes one of the fundamental theorems dealing with triangles if it suits him

[1] We have not yet touched upon the question whether the state
ought to care for the happiness of its members, for the concept of
happiness as such has no place in ethics, although our previous
investigations have taught us that good deeds do in fact bring
happiness, or rather joy (p. 29). The fact that we are aware of the
attendant joy does not cause an action to be non-ethical, so long as
it is not a motive in itself. Now it is equally a fact that a good state
makes happy the reasonable ones among its citizens. But those who
are happy and contented are better able to unfold their powers than
those who are discontented, and thus it is perfectly permissible for
the state to be aware that it can bring happiness to its citizens by
means of good laws. Only this knowledge must not be a motive.

To condemn happiness and joy as such would have a meaning
only if we knew that such a condemnation alone could lead to a
certain magical salvation. But this we do not know. On the other
hand, we do know that happiness serves to unfold powers and talents.
We must then allow it to exist. It is one of the many special tasks of
the state to see to it that it is not abused by slackers. It is a task that
can be solved completely, or at any rate very nearly.

and brings him gain. This is the place of all those who practise *Realpolitik*, and the only excuse that can be brought forward in their favour is that they have not clearly thought about what they were doing, apart from a few truly wicked persons. In fact they were practising no thorough-going *Realpolitik*, but one which is very one-sided and narrow. For moral sense, too, is a very real thing, and is even the most real thing of all in human nature. It is a sign of the harmony of the world in the moral sense that no man ever practised *Realpolitik* (in the ordinary sense of the word) and had lasting success in his enterprises if these infringed the elementary moral law.

If men refuse to listen to Jesus they should at least listen to the doctrines of men of such different bent as Tolstoy, Bertrand Russell, and F. W. Förster, without being offended by their occasional exaggerations. Germans especially ought to confess freely and without shame that Kant is a member of this great company.

(a) War

So long as there are more states than one single state, individual states ought to come to agreements by means of treaties reached as the result of reciprocal persuasion and accommodation. So far these methods have unfortunately been practised in a very limited extent, especially with respect to accommodation; nor have states hesitated, when it suited them, to have recourse to the least permissible of all political means, namely, to war—that is, to a systematic process of rendering the enemy defenceless; a process which differs from murder in that the killing of the enemy is not expressly intended, although it is unavoidable, as is perfectly well known to everybody. The argument that it is not intended to kill but only to render defenceless is a wretched subterfuge, to use the Kantian expression, since everybody knows that a shell or poison gas will kill with absolute certainty.

The whole of war from the beginning is wrapped in a dense shroud of words, which is ever a danger for clear ethical insight. It has its own vocabulary, with words like "battle", "to fall", "in the field", and, the most significant of all, the word "war" itself, whence arises the belief that that which is denoted by these words must be something of essential and elementary force in the world, something which accordingly is inevitable; whereas in fact most of these words have been coined in order to denote something that is rare or of merely practical significance. "Earthquake", "storm", "splinter", are far from being elementary. It is, then, important from the very beginning to break the spell of words (to give it a compendious designation) which frequently holds bound (for example) Hegel and his disciples. In the first instance words are no more than words, and in each instance an exact examination of the facts is required to determine whether they are of merely practical significance, or whether they denote some essential factor of the world.

After these preliminary remarks we proceed to work.

K

We know that in certain definite cases an apology may be offered for killing, namely, where it is an immediate means of defence, either of self, or, more especially, of others.

There is, then, one form of war in favour of which this apology may be admitted in advance. If some well-ordered constitutional community is attacked by hordes, of which it is known that they will slaughter the inhabitants if they prove victorious, then it is permissible to kill these hordes in war, although it is certain that all this *ought* not to be. This, however, is the sole instance where war proper or some similar mass-undertaking, for example the organized defence of a town or farm against savages, is permissible: and fortunately it is hardly ever realized for so-called modern civilized mankind. To-day war is declared or promoted indirectly against states of which it is known that its members would *not* slaughter or murder.

Practically, then, war must to-day be absolutely avoided, even as a means for defending neutrality. There are means to which moral approval may be accorded which are far more efficacious, like passive resistance and boycott. When an injury is inflicted, and it proves impossible to reach an agreement by peaceful means, recourse should be had to these.

Let us assume that an enemy comes, quite without moral justification, extorting every kind of concession, and even occupying territory. He should be suffered to act as he will; only obedience should be refused; ill should be endured for the sake of ethical purity. The enemy will soon realize his position, and will understand that the part which he is playing is ridiculous; and that is the worst injury that can be inflicted upon his heroic rôle.

I now proceed to marshal the reasons against war. All the reasons here are based upon reflection and not upon cognitive instinct (p. 60), for war is an undertaking agreed upon in advance, and all the relations there subsisting are relations between man and man.

It is true that the capital reason to be urged against war is based upon a rule which is already in existence and regulates human relationships in a fundamental manner. It is this: "Thou shall not kill" (p. 97), because the very meaning of death is unknown. Priority belongs to this rule. More general considerations have already made us acquainted with it, and we know that it has the rank of an axiom and admits of no infringement.

Talents may be destroyed in the course of a war, the development of which would be to the advantage of all, even to that of the destroyer. This is the second argument, which, like the first, results from an axiom, or at any rate a pseudo-axiom. Perhaps in the latest great war a Beethoven fell on the German side, a Descartes on the French, and a Newton on the English. This is a terrible thought. Surely a noble-minded Frenchman must regret the victory of his country, not only when he thinks of the potential Descartes, but also when he thinks of the potential Beethoven: and surely a noble-minded German must rejoice that he was not victorious when he thinks that a possible victory might have been purchased at the cost of the death of a potential Descartes or Newton.

In the third place we may advance the enormous economic damage which war generally inflicts upon all, even upon the victorious side—the argument of "The Great Illusion".

The objection may, however, be made that the preservation of the state has priority over everything personal, since the state is a supra-personal *ens*. It is not so, for the state is not a supra-personal *ens*; it is an accidental product of history, and ethically is not an end but a means.

Even the great single state, if it existed, would be no more than a means to an end. Why then should my individual state serve as a universal justification—the state which is an intermediate something between the individual person and the single community of all mankind? Here surely the family would be a more natural intermediate term; yet what would be said of a system of family morals which made itself superior to the general axioms of ethics? Men ought to think for themselves, and should not allow themselves to be led by conventions or Hegelian doctrines which they accept uncritically.

The state exists for the individuals and for their ethical well-being: we may say figuratively that the individuals have made it for themselves. This their creature is designed to react upon them, and the real aim is to bring about a certain state within themselves—the ethical state. Here we must not confuse the means with the end.

The insignificance of all that appertains to the individual state, and hence of so-called political history, is best understood if we turn our eyes away from the familiar history of the West. For centuries bloody wars have been waged between the various Indian states, the various Chinese states, and between Burmese and Siamese; and without ceasing great states have declined in Asia, and small states grown great. Most Europeans, even those whose education is pretty complete, know nothing of all this. But we have never felt the lack of this knowledge in our picture of the world, and it is changed in no way after we have acquired this knowledge. No better testimony can be found of the insignificance of war and politics.

It is wholly indifferent whether a state grows greater or less. All that matters is that it shall be good. Of course, it is immoral in the highest sense if state A robs state B of part of its territory merely because it chooses to do so. But one immoral action does not cancel another, but only increases the sum of immoral actions. The aggressor has acted immorally: let it be so. In no case must we reply with ideas of revenge.

It goes without saying that the case is altered if some part of a state, some province or district, wishes to leave the body politic to which it has belonged hitherto because the population so desires it from reasons like peculiarity of language or customs. The dissidents may wish to form part of another state or to found a new one, and in either case they should be suffered to go their way:

ethics demand it, and the lot of the diminished state will be happier without the unwilling member. Matters are different again, unfortunately, where there are within one district populations mixed either in race or in language. Here there can be no cleavage: the minority must yield, and the majority should show magnanimity. This ideal has been realized in Switzerland, and a League of Nations could realize it for the world.

It has been urged in favour of war that it offers opportunities for heroism and sacrifice of self for others. Certainly this is true with generous men, and there are professional officers who live in this thought alone. Even if we do not share their views we must refrain from judging these men. But to an equal, and probably to a greater, extent war offers an opportunity to the lust of cruelty and the love of adventure, a phenomenon which we have witnessed everywhere as a consequence of the Great War. And further, surely nobody wishes for earthquakes and conflagrations, although these, too, offer occasions for self-sacrifice and heroism.

It may be objected that war is sublime. Those who make this assertion perhaps have dashing cavalry attacks in mind rather than trenches and poison gas. Let us at least hope so, and let us readily admit the sublimity of these attacks, and perhaps also of modern air combats. But have we a right to wish for these forms of war because they are sublime? We ask once more: Does anybody wish for earthquakes and conflagrations? These, too, are sublime.

Aestheticism, alas, is both an easy and a superior pose.[1]

Perhaps it may be objected to our almost wholly uncompromising rejection of war that a certain impulse for self-preservation and even for domination is instinctive in man, and that we have already allowed instincts to be "cognitive"—that is, that we have allowed them to set the course of our ethical actions.

We are quite ready to admit that the instinct just mentioned shall be allowed this directive function. But surely it will be preserved from the crudest form in which it can manifest itself, which precisely is killing, by the *instinct* which leads us to feel disgust at killing. And further, man also has given to him that which may be called reflecting reason; and reason teaches him all the objections against war which we have been enumerating.

Certainly the instinct of self-preservation has the right of free play; but it must remain under the domination of reason.

We condemn war because it is something anti-ethical. For this we have two grounds: the axioms of elementary ethics, which are supposed to have binding force even when they are no more than pseudo-axioms; and the realization, reached by reflection, that the individual state (1) is an accidental product of history, and no new *ens* standing over against the totality of mankind, and

[1] The preference for national costumes cherished by many should fall under the same kind of condemnation. Heaven preserve us from wearing them ourselves—but the common people may do so. I am here reminded of a saying of an Italian colleague, who wittily remarked during a debate about national costumes: "L'uomo non è fatto per abbellire il mondo."

(2) is never more than a means towards the realization of ethical ends. Briefly, then, the individual state is nothing divine, but only serves the realization of the divine. Hence it must never act contrarily to the very foundations of that which it serves, namely, the axioms of ethics.

This view would be refuted, or at any rate would become doubtful, if it could be demonstrated that the individual state as such is a peculiar *ens* of a supra-personal kind. If this were the case, and then only, a new axiom could enter into ethics and modify the former axiom. But there is no reason whatever for making this assumption; and accordingly our theory is not only not invalidated, but has not even reached a "point of dichotomy" (p. 74).

In former times wars were waged whose alleged justification was not indeed that the individual state is something divine, but still that it was some kind of higher *ens*, and such wars might still be waged although in practice they have ceased. But, as we have already said, this higher *ens* is not the individual state, but something wholly different, so that even those wars of the past fail to justify war in favour of the individual state. Indeed, these wars were not that which to-day goes under the name of war.

I am here thinking of the so-called holy war. It is not a state-action, but an action of a semi-religious and a semi-metaphysical nature. In passing we may remark that torture as used by the Inquisition was of a similar nature.

The holy war, too, ought not to be; but the dualism of the world makes it possible to offer an apology for it. For those who wage this war it is no less than a duty, provided, of course, that it is waged solely for the sake of the sacred cause, that is, in order to achieve salvation from eternal damnation. In that case "supreme pity" is manifested in it: a few are killed in order that a far greater number may be saved for that which is meta-physically supreme. (The nature of this is supposed to be known.) The first crusade and the first wars of the Mohammedans may perhaps be interpreted in this way. On the other hand the wars which followed the French and the Russian revolutions do not, of course, belong to this class, for the only ideal which can justify and even make imperative a holy war is the unearthly ideal. Future political and social ideal states, even if their realization is seriously believed in, remain earthly ideals.

In our day nobody seriously holds the only beliefs which would justify a holy war. The apologists of national wars sometimes wear a religious cloak of a similar nature (Fichte and Hegel offer them numerous arguments): but that is an attitude with which we need not concern ourselves.

War in the only form in which it can occur to-day stands ethically condemned.

A word remains to be said about one form of war which might perhaps take place in the future, although it would be best if it were never to take place, and that is a war waged by the League of Nations against a state that has broken the peace. Even this kind of war evidently *ought* not to be, and as long as possible boycotting and the cutting off of supplies should be used as means of persuasion. But in our opinion the war waged by the League of Nations must be counted as admitting of apology, since it would be something after the nature of action by the police, which still remains to be discussed.

The pacifists have often been charged with not offering any substitute for the war-like virtues, and no field in which those qualities of the soul can have play, the nobility of which is admitted even by the enemies of war. We have already briefly mentioned these qualities.

Is it true that there is no substitute? Surely in this dualistic world there is an enormous number of fields, labour in which is advantageous and *good* for the community, and for the labourer full of danger. Such is the work of the doctor in the tropics, or at times when an infectious disease is raging; that of the sailor, the aviator, the miner, and the labour which is involved when virgin lands are put under the plough and rendered habitable so that settlers can dwell and make their living on them. In sciences, too, there are experiments which are as dangerous as they are necessary.

It is here that the man who is born a hero can show his mettle, quite apart from those great disasters which occur almost every year in some part of the world. Or, finally, such a man can volunteer for the police forces or those of the League of Nations.

It seems to me that this uncertain world always offers opportunities to the would-be hero.—To the genuine hero honour is due.

(β) War-Guilt

We will now pursue in somewhat greater detail the theory of war, since it is of such far-reaching importance for the present day.

For it would seem as though in our day at long last considerations of the ethics of war might have some chance of ethical realization.

It is a curious fact that to-day all those who have had a share in the war raise the question of war-guilt. The fact that nobody will admit that the fault lay with him is ethically satisfactory, for it shows that at bottom all consider war to be wicked.

Bertrand Russell has expressed some profound truths about war. He says somewhere that no evil which we seek to avoid by means of war is a greater evil than war itself. With this opinion we fully concur, although in contrast to the English thinker we take it rather in an ethical and not in an economic-practical sense. He goes on to say that wherever war breaks out all concerned are to blame.

That is the truth; it has been the fault of all, though none will admit it.

If we wish to speak of guilt we must, of course, begin by determining what we mean by it. In the highest sense there can be guilt only on the assumption that the activity of the soul (or, at any rate, the part of it which we call ego) is free. By freedom we mean further, as we know already (pp. 23, 24), that the quality of an action, or at any rate its realization—that is, the admission of a content of will into realization—is not conditioned by an unchanging *nature* which lies at the bottom of it, this nature being what might be called a permanent factor. It is rather assumed that man, in similar circumstances and having the same previous history, can act either in the sense of A or of non-A. Now, as we know, the question of freedom in the strictest sense admits of no solution, or at any rate none has ever been found. Hence every question of guilt in the profoundest sense cannot be, or at any rate has never been, solved.

But there is another kind of guilt: that of which we are made aware when our ethical intuition leads us to say of something that it *ought not to be*, this assertion being made without any reference to the metaphysical question of freedom; it is sufficient for ethical theory (p. 24) that something ought not to be.

In this narrower sense of pure intuition those are guilty of a war whose actions ought not to have been, precisely because they led to the war: it is here indifferent whether these persons could have acted differently or not. In this sense, all those who are concerned in a war are guilty.

Three conditions must exist in order that any event shall happen: the original cause must operate, a state of susceptibility to the cause must exist, and the conditions must exist which render possible the existence of the former two, and hence of the effect.

The original cause here is the declaration of war. The state which declares war, whether from intellectual clumsiness—without consciously intending harm or perhaps only from fear, is guilty in the same way in which a person is guilty of causing a stain on the carpet if he was clumsy enough to knock over an inkpot—even if somebody else had previously placed the inkpot at a particularly dangerous spot on the table. (In that case, the other person, too, is guilty.) All the other states which are concerned in the war are also guilty, because their governments accepted the declaration of war, and did not confine themselves to passive resistance; for even defensive wars are forbidden.

But there is something more important, and that is the general constellation of events and the state of mind which alone allows the declaration of war and its acceptance to become effective. It is quite thinkable that one government should declare and the other accept the declaration of war, but that the peoples should refuse to take part. Here those are guilty who do their share in developing the mentality which renders war possible, and even those who watch its development without opposing it, and above all those who, being members of a government, did not hinder by means of penalties the fostering of the militaristic frame of mind. As a matter of empirical fact whenever a war broke out there have been parties and individuals in the belligerent nations who under the cloak of patriotism fostered a warlike frame of mind and prepared wars and drove men into them by their praises of war. In practice no government will either declare or accept a declaration of war unless it knows that it has the bulk of the people behind it. Consequently there have been in each country people who were guilty of war because they prepared the war-mentality; and since in every country the governments did not hinder such persons in their evil work by means of punishment, all governments are guilty a second time, quite apart from declarations of war, and acceptance of and reply to it.

It is unreasonable for a people which has waged a war to declare its innocence, and it is equally unreasonable to place the sole guilt of a war upon one single people. At bottom indeed a people as a whole is never guilty of a war: logically there are only some of them who are guilty, and in fact these are not numerous. In the last analysis probably there is only a handful of men who drew the rest with them, and that chiefly by means of suggestion. This handful in turn consists partly of those who actually caused the war and of those who created the mentality favouring it. In future we must be on our guard against these few.

In medicine, prevention is counted more important than cure. Hence the first task of a moral government in the struggle against the development of a militaristic mood is the punishment and suppression of any words which might serve to irritate or to ridicule other nations.

It is fashionable to speak of the hatred between the

peoples, and there are even individuals who preach this hatred. I myself have never understood this hatred, and, what is more, I have never found it even among those who glorify it; and that is good, for hatred would be infra-human. What I have discovered was anger at a defeat on the one side and lust in power following upon victory on the other. But I venture to assert that every human being, even those who preach hatred, would extend their help to an enemy citizen if he were to fall into their hands weak or ill, apart from some few cases of moral insanity, which are bound to occur here and there. This would probably not happen with genuine hatred, which is virtual murder, and fortunately is almost as rare as real murder. Let us, then, rejoice that this at least does not take place, and let us spare ourselves that silly talk of hate, which more carefully looked at is, fortunately, no more than a bombastic phrase, but nevertheless a rather harmful phrase. We should not make ourselves out to be worse than we are.

(γ) *Conscription, Police, etc.*

If war ought not to be, then any institution that has war for aim ought to be prohibited by law.

In the first place I have here in mind so-called conscription, an arrangement which was adopted during the last war even by those states which hitherto had been immune from this disease—a fact much to be regretted from the ethical point of view. So-called conscription—that is, if we wish to speak without hypocrisy, compulsory service—is to be condemned not only because it is a preparation for war, but for two other reasons as well. The first is, that by means of it such persons as do not wish to kill or to learn to kill are forced to kill. In states with mercenary armies the sin, when war breaks out, lies at least only with the governments and the mercenaries; but in states with conscription all are by law compelled to sin. In the second place it is contrary to the dignity of man to compel him to a line of action which lies outside general human necessities of life, against his wish, or at any rate without consulting him. There might be some excuse for compulsory agricultural labour, but not for compulsory military service. Kant's saying, that man must never be used as a means to an end, has here a particularly significant meaning. There is an insult to human dignity even in military drill if a man does not submit to it voluntarily.

Tolstoy once said that all human ills come from the military caste. That is an overstatement, for there are evils which are not due to it, and in a special form the military profession, unfortunately, as we shall soon see, is necessary and justifiable. But it is true that in the form which it has normally had hitherto it has been the cause of evil.

Where there is no danger of attacks from savages, there a police force may be admitted if not actually justified for the purpose of maintaining the peace within, since in practice it is unfortunately a necessity. No man should be compelled to serve in this force, since killing might become a necessity. On the other hand, those who volunteer for such a force should have our full respect, for the reason that they voluntarily take sin upon themselves in the shape of killing, at least potentially. The sins of all are concentrated upon one man: and this he knows and wills.

We said above (p. 154) that a war waged by the League of Nations is at bottom no war, but analogous to police action, so that fundamentally it is an internal affair of the state. For a true League of Nations would be one single state in the profoundest sense. Thus all that has been said about the nature of a police force also applies to the members of the future army of the League of Nations. Respect is due to its members, but membership ought to be free.

A few words must be said about the relation between readiness for war and propagation within the state. It has been asserted that women ought to bear as many children as possible because the king needs soldiers. Here there is a perfect abyss of moral aberration; the child is degraded to be a mere unit in a mass, and the mother, to be a machine for producing the material that is to be used in order to kill and to be killed. To pursue this any further would lead us into a depth which is contrary to the dignity of this book: we therefore return to ethically serious matters.

A law, then, which demands conscription has morally no binding force, any more than a law would have which were to compel the whole of the population to marry in order to breed the greatest possible number of soldiers. For the rest, it might be possible to argue that there is an obligation to marriage—were it not that asceticism, too, is a possible moral doctrine. The state is not of sufficient importance to have the right of interference in moral consciousness, which is a wholly personal matter.

It may be asked why I do not enter upon the moral value of various instruments of war—that is, upon the methods of waging war in their details. I do not do so because the prohibition of the genus implies the prohibition of the species. It is not the task of general ethical theory to assign degrees of infamy within the general class of infamous actions; and I am even tempted to consider such a proceeding particularly offensive because it surrounds the infamy of war with the cloak of right, while the infamies which are indignantly condemned are merely derivative. All the horrors which our generation has experienced—the invasion of neutral territories, the starvation of old men, women, and children, poison gas and aerial bombs, are insignificant compared with the fundamental fact that in war men are organized to oppose one another, having received the best training in order to aim, to fire, and to stab, and all for the sake of the state. I openly confess that at the outbreak of the Great War, it was my own hope, as well as that of a great number of the enemies of war, that at the last moment noble youths might be horrified in numbers at the sin which they were being asked to commit, and would thus render the war impossible. Our hope was deceived this time, if we except the attitude taken up by certain groups among the Anglo-Saxon and Russian peoples. Nevertheless it still remains our hope and even our firm faith.

I also refrain from discussing so-called colonial wars and the acquisition of colonies in general, since the whole of this question has already been settled by implication. The forcible domination of foreign races is equally non-moral, even when it complacently cloaks itself under the pretence of "education."

Thus in the profoundest sense war can never be justified. Formerly an apology might be offered for a holy war, and it can still be offered for a war against savages. But there is no other war for which so much as an apology can be offered: war is no better than deliberate and organized killing, which, just because it is organized, is far worse than murder committed under the influence of passion or need.

In spite of this there are men who approve of war, although both their education and their general disposition is good in the ordinary affairs of life. This approval is due to their lack of education and their ignorance in ethical matters. We shall have to speak further about this curious state of affairs, and at this point we confine ourselves to saying that to-day there is absolutely nothing that is of equal importance with the definitive abolition of war based upon profound ethical intuition. Compared with the question of pacifism, all economical and even all social questions take second rank: for here we are concerned with an axiom. Those who have not yet acquired a purely ethical manner of thinking, and are still engaged in "economic" ways of thought, should not forget that the great harmony of the world causes a wicked action to be also a stupid one: nor should they forget the teaching of history, which shows that every conqueror in turn became conquered; for that which was born by force perished by force. Let us at long last make a new kind of history.

(δ) *Patriotism and its Manifestations*

The concept of culture as opposed to civilization is peculiarly German. I can assert from personal experience that other peoples often fail to grasp what we wish to denote by this distinction.

It seems to me that we mean in Germany by "civilization" the totality of the arrangements of a state by means of which human labour is made easier—that is to say, in the last analysis, is economized. By culture we mean the totality of supreme personal achievements of a scientific and an artistic kind, together with their reflection upon other persons who themselves are not creators. Now the state as such can concern itself about the whole of its civilization; but as far as culture is concerned it can do no more than create a spirit of receptivity for the efforts of those persons who do the true work of culture, and prepare the ground for such efforts. The efforts themselves are wholly personal, and as such are beyond the influence of any outside factor.

A state which does its best to foster civilization and the requisites of culture is a good state, a state as it ought to be, and it deserves the respect of its citizens and their active devotion. Man is a ζῷον πολιτικόν—that is, a being which by its nature has the capacity to form states, and here he should give unrestricted play to this capacity; and even in a bad state he ought to give it full play in order to make this state good.

For the state, whether it be single or one of many, although it is no more than a means, is still a very powerful means towards morality.

But we must not forget that it is no more than a means: we must and can respect it to the highest degree, but we cannot venerate (or, as is usually said, "love") it, but only the end at which it aims.

This leads us to the question of so-called love of country or patriotism.

In order to love I must have an accurate knowledge of the object of my love. Thus I can and do love my own country; any injunction to do so is superfluous, and consequently meaningless. Any region and community of men in which I have sojourned for a long time can be my country: with the majority of mankind this will be their native country. A great obstacle which prevents the majority of men from having many more countries than one lies in the variety of languages. A certain idleness and sloth may here conduce to dangerous narrowness.

Love of country simply exists: it has no aim but love, seeks after nothing else and asks after nothing else. As love it is perfectly good.

Now this love has been applied to the state, and in this connection the term "patriotism" has been coined. Many men regard it as taboo, and yet it is infinitely ambiguous, and hence dangerous.

That man is a rogue who does not rejoice to promote the welfare of his state to the best of his ability even against his personal wishes; but very often he is a sinner unawares, if he loves it in the manner in which a mother loves her child, excusing and even defending those parts of it which are immoral.

Every man should have respect for the state, if only because even the worst of states implies at least a certain minimum of order: and a little is better than nothing when we are dealing with something that is fundamentally good. I have even the right to *love* my own state when it seeks to embody some particularly ethical idea, and in a certain measure succeeds in doing so. Here not only love of country but even patriotism is justified (love is by nature such that it can never be exacted): a love which, as we hinted above, is given not so much to the state as such as to the ideal at which it aims and to the community of men who have made this ideal theirs. Hence this love is best called a loving sense of fellowship. There are very few states which consciously make the pursuit of an ideal their aim. The aims of most are exclusively of an economical order, and therefore demand no more than respect; and many which have an ideal seek to attain it by objectionable means.

We have already said above that it is indifferent in a state whether it is great or little, and that all that matters is that it shall be good.

Much is said about the honour of the state: it is said that it must be defended by force of arms; and this is one of the main excuses advanced for war.

What is this honour? And what is honour with the individual person? Really Schopenhauer has said all that can be said, and I have not the illusion that in these paragraphs I am advancing anything original.

Honour is the totality of the modes in which I exist as a spiritual person in so far as this totality of modes is based upon my good actions; it deserves respect just in so far as these actions were good. I have preserved my dignity, and consequently I have a claim to be honoured: that is to say, I have a personal honour. Now first of all it is clear that my honour can be stained only by my own future actions, and not by anything that some other person does to me. If he does me harm, he stains his own honour and not mine. To assert the opposite, as is done by those who defend the practice of duelling, is the most unthinking kind of conventionalism. Did Jesus lose his honour by what he suffered others to inflict upon him, as we read in the gospels? Yet the defenders of the so-called code of honour should assert this if they wish to be consistent.

We will now apply the concept of honour to the state. Here too it is true that its honour can be injured only by that which it does, and not by that which it suffers and calmly endures. Its honour is the totality of its empirical morality, that is to say, the totality of the *good* which stands to its credit, and which is the result of its labours in the interests of civilization and culture. It is the justified consciousness of its dignity. And here, if foreign states inflict injury upon injury on it, it may justly say: "Let it all go, their profit shall be small, the Kingdom of God remaineth"—that is, the kingdom of the ethical world, of which the state is a member in so far as it is good.

Any state which in any way seeks to inflict violence of any kind upon another does injury to its own honour. For the state never has the right to seek its own interests at the expense of another.

This is the parting of the ways for the two forms of patriotism which are empirically given us. The one form tells us: The state must be respected without any reservation as being the highest moral means, and a man must wholly serve his own state, since that is the state to which he happens to belong. And this state should even be loved, if in fact it realizes a certain idea, which is peculiar to it and has an ethical content which exacts love. But merely because it is my state I have no right to think that it is better than others, nor must it infringe the rights of other states nor inflict upon them the very slightest injury. This is true patriotism, or reverence for the state coupled with love. Nobody could be more insistent upon this doctrine than the author.

The other form says: My state before all, and the others do not interest me. At best this is love—a blind love where only critical respect is in place. More frequently it is no better than a veiled selfishness, which is made no better, but morally worse, by the fact that it allows a man to hide, together with others who hold similar sentiments, behind the word of patriotism, and has not the courage to confess itself for what it is. My own state is to be great and powerful and feared, and it is to grow greater and more powerful by means of force, in order that I shall be able to feel that I have a power at the back of me and am one to whom no man dares do injury even by word. At the same time I am far from being an egoist. Strange that this same patriotism is the object of abuse and sarcasm whenever it is found particularly well developed in another people.

What we have here before us is false patriotism, which ought always to be called by its right name of Jingoism or nationalism. Those who work on its behalf are digging the grave of culture and ethics. This patriotism is a sin, and unless we soon succeed in overcoming it in Europe, we shall be faced deservedly by a veritable *Decline of the West*. If no other patriotism were possible except this, which is at once that of the bully and of the coward, then it would be best that country and patriotism were lost in the deepest depths of hell.

But such is not the case. Patriotism can have another

form, as we know, namely, that of simple love for country and of grave respect before the state. In this form patriotism *may* not only, but *ought* to, be.

The distinction which we have drawn can also be applied if we make use of the word "pride". If pride is the quiet, humble, and thankful conviction that I have preserved intact my moral dignity, and if it involves no insolence towards others, then I have the right to be proud and also to feel proud—that is, to feel an inner satisfaction—at being a member of a good state. But if pride is to make a man a bully, whether by reason of his own strength or that of the state, then it is immoral and at the same time ridiculous. Here Schopenhauer's saying is true, that national pride is the most ridiculous kind of pride; and the other saying too of this great man is true: "Every nation laughs at every other nation, and they all are right."

But there is another kind of pride, which is a quiet and not a boastful satisfaction at one's own achievements and those of the state to which a man belongs, and upon the permanent improvement of which he consciously and seriously co-operates; and this kind of pride is not ridiculous, but wholly justified. For nature has given to man a feeling of dignity, and it works in him like an instinct.

(d) WORK WITHIN THE STATE

(a) *General Considerations*

Each man's work within the state must tend to make it progressively and continuously a better moral institution.

In the first place any immoral elements in it are to be removed; in the second place new and positive moral elements should be added to those which are already in existence.

Now that slavery and torture have been abolished, all our efforts in the first sense must be directed towards the abolition of war; and this conviction has been the reason why, in our theory of ethics, we entered upon the question of war in particular detail. As a political measure, war ought to be counted morally impossible, out of the question and infra-human, as much as torture would be considered out of the question, for any body of judges, even if they were convinced of the guilt of the accused and would give anything to possess a statement from him.

The fact that so-called pacificism has spread so widely in all countries, finding a visible expression in the League of Nations, is in fact tantamount to an entry into a new ethical era. It is an exceedingly slow process; but this fact must not deter those who have been enlightened by pity from co-operating to the best of their power. Scientific knowledge too comes slowly; but still any good piece of individual work serves to promote it. All those who feel that they are citizens of this new

age should attempt before all to act upon the new generation, and to fill it with the conviction that military fame
as such confers no honour, although in individuals this
fame may have been earned by heroic sacrifice. Great
harm has here been done by scholastic institutions;
they ought to undo this harm, and they have the power
to do so. Gravely and impressively they ought to explain
even to the youngest that it is wicked to vilify other
nations and to indulge in a bullying patriotism; and the
best means of doing this is to show the terrible consequences. It should be preached to them in a spirit of
humility, that we are all one spirit. And if another nation
is possessed by the devil of power and does violence
to our own, they ought to be taught to feel not hate but
pity for those others who are doing hurt to their own
honour and dignity. Such doctrines should be taught
more especially in the history lessons: a history, not of
wars, but of the noblest achievements of culture should
be taught. In Germany Treitschke should not be taught,
nor Hegel, nor the later doctrine of Fichte, but Schlosser,
Schopenhauer, and Fichte's earlier doctrine.

(β) Cosmopolitanism and Particularism. The League of Nations

The pacifist who has a clear grasp of the ethical postulates
is a cosmopolitan to this extent, that the ultimate social
condition at which he aims is one single state; mankind
to him is a union of all men who live together in peace

and justice, and approaching as nearly as possible to moral purity. It is true that this community will probably have to exist in the form of a state so long as it is earthly.

But the pacifist as cosmopolitan does not for that reason wish to suppress the individualities of groups of men formed by nature and history, and to put in their place a general average. His aim is a culture which is to be essentially of the same nature with all, but is to have a peculiar form with each race. He even goes further than those who to-day call themselves nationalists. He does not aim at the German or the French type, for these forms are too artificial, and are not wholly valid. He is a particularist, and the type at which he aims is that of the Rhineland, of Baden, Saxony, and the Hanse towns on the one side, and that of Brittany, Lorraine, and Arles on the other. All these are to seek to excel one another in pacific rivalry, as is done to-day by students and artists and by the bodies consisting of them. On the other hand, if this should prove impossible, and if it were inevitable that particularistic bodies based upon cultural peculiarities should enter into strife and war, then it would be better to put up with the average or general melting-pot. It would still be better than war. But the cosmopolitan-particularistic pacifist has the faith that this will not be so.

It may be even that he has before him as ideal, at least for Europe, to disintegrate the nations of this continent into the good old regions and provinces of the old style, and then to proceed to form one great federation of Baden, Württemberg, Hanover and the rest, of Burgundy,

Provence, Piedmont, Campania, Tuscany, Andalusia, Castile, and many others, this federation to have one capital and to form one state. For the moment, however, we are content to hope that the existing nations will unite to form one single state.

Economically, too, this state of course would be a single unit. Customs barriers would exist only in the dictionary. It goes without saying that a supreme court of judicature and an executive police force would have to be instituted.

Within the nations as they exist to-day the various territories and even the towns once had their own Customs barriers; they looked upon each other enviously as competitors, and even waged war upon one another. If it has been possible to unite them into a small number of nations, why should it not be possible to go one step further and unite the nations into a single political and economic unit? In that case the nations would have fulfilled their purpose as transitional stages on the way to the ecumenical man. If they are looked upon as something more than transitional stages they are ethically mere impediments.

The central authority of a state would have to confine itself, however, almost exclusively to tasks of civilization: it would have to concern itself with post office, telegraphs, railways, and police. Culture would belong to the provinces, and perhaps this might also apply to the administration of the law with the exception of a supreme court for certain legal points.

That alone would be a true League of Nations. It may be objected that it would mean the loss of sovereign rights for the existing states. There seems to be no harm in that, however, since the loss would be borne by all states alike, and that is a small thing compared with the possibility of a lost war and a restriction in sovereignty dictated by the conqueror.

All that has here been said with regard to Europe represents, of course, no more than a first and preliminary step. Heaven preserve us from creating in Europe a single power of vast resources which would then proceed to make war upon a united Asia or America! Our aim is a single state having for territory the whole earth: Pan-Europe is a necessary preliminary stage in a process whose aim from the beginning is a Pan-Cosmos.

It must not be objected here that the different nations cannot ever understand one another, and that they think, feel, and will in an altogether different manner. This simply is not the truth. The Germans enjoy Michael Angelo and Dante, Calderon and Velasquez, Descartes, Pascal, and Bizet, Shakespeare and Hume; and, in France, those with whom alone we are here concerned, the educated class, are familiar with Kant, Goethe, Beethoven, Wagner, and Nietzsche.

These observations have been restricted to the educated class. It will now be said that the common people are believed even by the author to be incapable of understanding other peoples and another state. In that case it will be necessary to educate the common people until they become "educated": after all, this is in any case a general moral task.

However, as has already been said, our state is not designed to make a halt at Europe. It will perhaps be said that surely this is a Utopia, and surely Europeans and Asiatics do not understand one another. Surely their ways of thinking are so different that it is possible to speak of a European, a Mohammedan, an Indian, and a Chinese truth.

(γ) *The Nature of Peoples. Can They understand One Another?*

This "truth", generally framed in somewhat nebulous and obscure terms, has succeeded in completely intoxicating a numerous class of the public. In fact, however, this is no truth. A complete lack of understanding can exist only as between cultured and primitive races, and even between these it *need* not exist in principle.[1] The doctrine that there is an insuperable difference existing in principle between the different views of the world which are characteristic of the several races of cultured peoples is certainly wrong. There are differences in the manner in which the mental dispositions are compounded in the various races, but these differences are quantitative and not qualitative; it is never the case that one kind of disposition does not exist at all in some race or other;

[1] Here, too, caution should be exercised. The American intelligence tests between Whites and Negroes are slightly, but not more than slightly, favourable to the former. For the rest, the same is also true of certain European nations, which I purposely refrain from naming in order not to arouse national squabbles.

and exactly the same differences may be found between the members of the same race.[1] The numerical proportion subsisting between "pure lines" differs in the different peoples, and that is all. This has been proved beyond all doubt by the intelligence tests which we have already mentioned on p. 138.

On the other hand, it must be admitted, in the first place, that among the civilized races some have more fully elaborated one side of the world-picture and others another side; and, in the second place, that the logical height to which this development has been carried (measured by those critical and logical standards which empirically have proved of universal validity) is at the moment different in the different civilizations.

I am writing the first draft of this book in China, and in daily close contact with the inhabitants. Here I find not the slightest degree of lack of mutual comprehension. I am lecturing on my own system and upon the history of modern European philosophy. The listeners pay the closest attention, and ask many exceedingly sensible questions and some few silly ones—just like German students.

I shall be told that these individuals form merely a small circle. That, I admit; but after all it consists of genuine Chinese. All that is necessary is that the small circle shall be made great: and the future will see this realized.

[1] This settles the question of the Jews, which has been made into a "problem" quite artificially. I know Jews of every possible political, ethical, and metaphysical shade of view: but *the* Jew is a mere abstract average bearing an intentionally negative note.

M

With Mohammedans and Hindoos it is less easy to reach an understanding than with the races of the extreme East, for the former two have religious limitations, while the latter are intellectually liberal and remarkably tolerant.

But even here, as appears in India more plainly from year to year, there is no permanent obstacle to complete mutual understanding.

We said above that there is no fundamental difference in the intellectual structure of the non-primitive races; the differences are to be found in the respective fields of vision, and in the critical height to which the world-picture has been elaborated.

Thus if, for example, we take the Indians, we shall find that they have intuited and pondered a great deal that is extremely sound in the sphere of psychology, and very little in the sphere of Nature. And that which they have intuited was intuited in a form that corresponds to the European vision of the Middle Ages.

What is needed here is simply instruction—that is, it is equally necessary for the East and the West that attention be directed to all that *can* be intuited, and all that is of the nature of a *problem*; and in the second place, and more particularly for the East, attention must be drawn to the method which alone will give a thorough and complete "vision"—that is, to logical instruction.

How is it possible that Hindoos and members of the races of the Far East can pursue their studies successfully in Europe?

Truth is one, the true world-picture is one, and it

has one form only of which it is true that it is the best. To this form "we" have reached the closest approximation, while it may be the case that Asiatics have more material in the sphere of psychology. *We* must acquire the material which we have not yet intuited, while *all* have need of the form which is ours, nor is this assertion a piece of European arrogance.

The primitive Chinese sees everywhere the activities of spirits and dragons. Will it be seriously asserted that this too is a true world-picture? The educated Chinese themselves do not assert this. It is not necessary for the European to be more Chinese (or Indian) than the Chinese (or Indians). There may be a grain of truth even in the stories of dragons and spirits, and we may take it for a disguised form of vitalism or para-psychology. (This also applies to the Indian Yoga doctrine.) In that case the disguise must be stripped off, as it must equally be stripped from Christian Science, which surely is anything but Asiatic: and that form of clothing must be assumed which most closely approximates to the truth, which is one. Now it is objectively certain that this form in intellectual matters is the European form, although this has become true only since Europe discarded dogmatic materialism.

In ethical matters, on the other hand, China is far nearer to the single truth than the West. The Chinese state is weak and full of confusion, and yet life runs with perfect smoothness because of the lofty nature of the fundamental view of family ethics.

The case of India is very similar. "Nationalism means that a whole nation is brought up to a narrow ideal which leads to moral degeneration and intellectual blindness" (Tagore). "The more lukewarm a man is in the cause of humanity, the less valuable he is as a patriot" (Gandhi).

Thus it is possible for East and West to understand each other, for in the last analysis both are the children of one father, and this father is the "Spirit". If this is true, it is even more true that the spirit is essentially one within the sphere of a single culture; for example, that of the Western type. It is wholly erroneous to preach that there is a German, a French, or a British "nature" which is more than an average which was accidentally produced in the course of history. This nature can be changed in the individual if he is transplanted into another people while he is young. Many Polish and French emigrants have become Germans as far as their subjective feeling goes; and the converse too is true. The fact is that their new nature is a genuine nature no more than was the nature of their ancestors. By a genuine nature I mean an inalterable form in which their actual existence is cast, this form being part of the plan of the universe.

Apart from climate, geographical formation and position, and other factors, among which may also be that of race, provided it is pure, that which determines the so-called nature of a people is that group of great individuals which consists of those men of superior gifts who happen to be born within its limits. Thus, for example, English philosophy has an empirical-sensuous character (to which we may add that there are a great many exceptions) simply because Locke, Berkeley, and Hume were very remarkable men who happened to be born in Britain, and because it so happened that these men tended towards empiricism—a statement which, further, is true only with modifications. If Leibniz had been born in England he would have given a different "nature" to English philosophy. For the rest, modern Hegelianism has its origins in Great Britain and in Italy.

William James rightly observed long ago: "Originality in men dates from nothing previous, other things date from it, rather",[1] and even went so far as to decline to allow that race, environment, and specific experiences had any influence whatever upon originality.

All that matters is the great men. These create the spiritual atmosphere, and this in turn gives rise to the *average*, into which, perhaps at a later time, another great man is born. He in turn is subjected to influence, and if this influence happens to act upon similar gifts in this new man, then the environments become still more strongly defined, in their capacity for exerting influence, to operate perhaps in turn upon another great man at a later time; and so the progress goes on.

We must therefore beware of intellectual rashness in speaking of "nature", and we must cease to construe a "nature" by the process of seizing upon a selected few from among the multitude of types without any detailed analysis of the facts.

[1] *A Pluralistic Universe*, 1920, p. 226.

After all that has been said it will be obvious that national characteristics in the everyday sense of the word are quite inessential details, and on the other hand we may state specifically that that which is really significant in the distinctions between different groups of men has little to do with the element of nationality and nothing at all with that of race. But really these distinctions are not logically essential, and all that is essential is the Spirit which is one. All the great founders of religions have seen this, and to-day there are many examples to prove its truth: the Roman Catholic Church, Islam, Buddhism, and Hindooism take notice of races and nations no more than do modern science, engineering, or music. In India, indeed, members of the same race become enemies (which is more than I can praise) when one is a Hindoo and the other a Mohammedan. The modern movement towards peace, too, is a unity which transcends nations and races in its merely economical, and, still more, in its profounder form. And where the spiritual element is really powerful, even language cannot hinder its action. Where its power is less great it may become an obstacle, just as geographical facts at one time were obstacles. But we may say that everywhere wherein philosophy, art, science, or religion any element of nationality or race becomes apparent, there human frailty is present, and the highest achievements possible to spirit are not reached. It will never become possible wholly to discard this frailty. Indeed, where the frailty is harmless, the attempt need not even be made to cast it off by force: the guiding rule is always to work positively and not negatively. On the other hand it is not right to make a virtue of necessity. If a man really seeks after the realization of the spirit, national and racial prejudices will become superfluous and drop off of their own accord.

I am well aware that all this has not a very modern ring. But what is modern is not necessarily true. At the moment the belief in "race" is particularly modern. Might it not be suspected of being a belated offspring of the Darwinian age, that epoch when man was treated exclusively as a zoological being? Darwinianism in the narrower sense is nowadays out of date with biologists. But the mass of mankind is always some fifty years behind the times, and this is true even of the body of educated persons who are not experts; Darwinianism stands to the modern belief in race in the same relation in which Voltaire and Rousseau stood to the French Revolution. The "zoological" map of Europe is one of its belated results.

The only distinctions which, at any rate empirically and not in a metaphysical sense, are of any importance as between men and groups of men, are those which are based upon the psychological types, which now at long last are being seriously investigated by men like Spranger, Scheler, Grünbaum, and, above all, by Jung. The number of such types is limited, and it is probable that in their ultimate foundation they are innate. But these types are the same in all the nations and races within which they occur, and a member of type A will "get on" much better with a member of the same type in another nation (provided that language presents no obstacle) than with a member of the type B or C of his own nation. In our own time mankind has had occasion to experience this more powerfully than ever before. Attempts to hide the fact behind sounding phrases are unavailing, since in the long run no untruth can stand.

Perhaps the fundamental types to which all others can be reduced are the man of power and the man of love, unless we prefer to classify in the more objective manner of Jung. In the last analysis even the types are no more than differences in the quantitative mixture of the elements of the spirit.

It is time that we were spared the remark, which is so popular to-day, that one and the same political constitution will not serve for all, since the different nations have different natures.

We know the truth about this nature, and we know that all men are of the nature of the spirit. It is true that we meet with different heights of culture, which are due to contingent historical circumstances; we do not demand a universal vote in countries where many cannot write or read. So much we have said already, and we have at the same time demanded that these persons be educated so that they shall be able to write and read.

But when a certain stage in culture has been reached there is only one possible political form, and only one which is ethically justified, and that is democracy.

Surely it must be obvious that a man thinks poorly

of his own people when he declares that it is not yet ripe or of age for democracy. The hope centred in a dictator by force must be given up or chaos will result. The word "democracy" must not be abused, nor must it be treated with contempt, unless it is clearly stated what is the meaning of the word and the object of the contempt. What we mean by democracy (pp. 136 *sqq.*) is the most genuine kind of democracy—that which leads to true aristocracy; it does not imply a constitution where each man has a voice in matters of which he understands nothing.

This is the most genuine form of the government of a people by its best members; and to-day all civilized nations are ripe for it.

There are two examples in the history of Western man which prove that a single spiritual community, knowing itself to be one, can exist between men who are different both in race and language. One example is furnished by the Christian Middle Ages (as well as by the Mohammedan Middle Ages), and the other by modern North America. The nature of American culture is uniform down to the slightest detail from Honolulu to New York, and from the Canadian frontier to Florida; and nothing could show us more clearly what opinion we should hold of the alleged "nature" of the peoples of Europe. Here environment has formed a new "nature", and this very fact proves that it neither was nor is a true "nature": for a *true* "nature" is not formed by environment. It is true that such a major cultural unit requires a common language besides the languages of the minor groups, and, indeed, the Middle Ages had such a language in Latin (and Arabic) while the Americans have it in English. In the Far East its place is taken by a uniform script which is read differently in the different languages. The united Europe which is on the way will, of course, need either a language or a script, and the united World-State will also stand in need of it. The language will be English, unless at some future time the idea of a universal artificial language is taken more seriously than it is at present. Perhaps the desired end might also be achieved by a common pictorial language spoken differently by the different peoples, after the manner of Chinese. We might here bear in mind the *characteristica universalis* which Leibniz devised, as well as the fact that in Music, Chemistry, and Mathematics a universal symbolism of this kind is already in existence.

National languages as such are good and certainly are to be encouraged. But they are sacred no more than nationalistic states, and must not be allowed to form an obstacle in the way of the attainment of the demands of Ethics.

(δ) *Conclusion*

Thus in principle there is nothing in the way of the single state. It is best realized in the form of a federation of provinces. The only difficulties are practical: it will take time to overcome them, but difficulties of this nature can be overcome. Of the two greatest European teachers of ethics one said, "You can because you ought"; and the other, "You ought because you can". Both are right; and similarly, when it is asked whether the primacy should belong to the will of the soul or to thought, a decision in favour of either is equally justified. For "ought" has a meaning only if there is a meaning in "can", and the good which "can" be—"ought" to be, since this is part of the definition of good.

At this point two warnings must be given.

The first is directed against the danger of a plurality of Leagues of Nations. This would give us the nationalistic states of our time in a magnified form, and that would be a worse thing even than the present nations, for such federations would be even more powerful, and a war between them would be far more terrible and destructive than one between nations. In the so-called World War we have just experienced a war not indeed between genuine federations, but still between bodies of Allies; and it was this precisely that made it so terrible.

All intermediate types of groups in the series of groups, other than those which have developed naturally out of the family, can very easily do more harm than good. The only good groups are those small ones which are immediately superior to the family, where each member knows, or at any rate knows something about, each other member. Strangely enough the intermediate groups of the present day offer the greatest scope to the bullying patriotic tub-thumper. The only groups which ought to exist are the smallest, or natural, groups, and the one supreme group; the former are, of course, supposed to be communities held together by love and not by a common egoism.

The second warning is directed against any attempts to realize a world-wide federation by means of one last war to end war. It is quite certain that such a war would not be the last war, and the state to which it gave rise would pass away as surely as everything else that owes its origin to war. That which is established by force, by "blood and iron", will be destroyed again by force. It was the fundamental error of all the politicians of the grand style that they failed to see this.

No; it is wrong to say that one more war—the war which happens to be advocated at the moment—ought to be, and after that no more; on the contrary it is this particular war which ought not to be, for if this war is avoided the preceding war will have been the last. The case is here the same as with some bad habit such as drink. If a man says: It does not matter for to-day; to-day will be the last time, and after that I will begin a new life— then it is certain that he will fail to-morrow as he failed to-day.

One thing, however, we can say with the fullest conviction to all those who desire true glory and honour for their people: the day is not far when the glory of the nation that refuses to enter into a war, and is ready to accept for the moment disadvantages of every kind from this refusal, will have a brighter lustre in history than the glory of all the battles from Marathon to the

Great War could confer. The greatest glory will belong to the nation which acts as pioneer in this matter. What is important is to make a beginning with a new ethical code, and to make an end of the apology which is satisfied to say that the others are no better than I.

Have I a right to sin because my neighbour sins?

In our day the greatest obstacle to the dissolution of the nationalistic states into provinces, and to their reunion in a single state, consists in a certain quasi-religious cloak under which aggressive patriotism and imperialism have cunningly covered themselves: a disguise which does not require true love of country and respect for the state.

The Church has lost its appeal, and in wide circles genuine religious feeling has ceased to exist. But, although they do not know it, men require some substitute, and accordingly they have enthroned those idols called Roma or Germania or Britannia or Gallia. They are not even aware of the profound blasphemy which such conduct involves.

Of these unconscious blasphemers many are quite honest. This is true, for example, of many officers. These men we should respect and instruct of the error of their way. If a genuine chauvinist honestly though wrongly looks at a national war in the same light as a religious war, then he is unenlightened from lack of vision, but nevertheless is ethically vastly superior to those who approve of war from economic reasons. Essentially he may even be a good man whose good disposition has been given a wrong direction, and as such he may be superior to those who are pacifists merely from personal motives. At an earlier point (p. 147), where we were treating of a more respectable economic pacifism which does not necessarily imply personal selfishness, we did not allow even to this form a decisive word when we were laying the foundations of our theory that peace is an ethical postulate.

Many, however, are not honest, but—like so many priests—they desire profit and power; and they know that they will best win over the masses (including many so-called educated persons) for their purposes if they give a pseudo-religious cloak to their intentions. A certain Frenchman who could look beyond the surface once said: "They say Alsace and they mean potash; they say Lorraine and they mean iron."

To the teacher of ethics this alliance between a brutal patriotism on the one hand and sanctimoniousness and a degradation of the loftiest of all feelings on the other is particularly offensive; and it is a particular source of sorrow to him when he sees it exerting its spell over numbers of men who are good and honest by nature but have no independent judgment.

What is needed above all, then, is enlightenment. In its genuine form it alone can put an end to a deification of the state, and clear the path for a new and true spirit of religion. We proceed, then, to speak of genuine enlightenment.

III

ENLIGHTENMENT

In our days the word "enlightenment" has become unpopular, and I am well aware that at the first glance this section will appear to most readers the most inopportune in a book the whole of which is inopportune to the times in which it appears. Nevertheless, I am full of hope as I write it; for I see on the one hand that a great many persons mean by "enlightenment" something which it is not, and I see on the other hand that a great many are enemies of true enlightenment only because they lack the power to attain it: they have proved unable to achieve enlightenment unaided, and accordingly, finding the battle vain, they have laid down their arms and have made terms with the darkness which surrounds them. Thus on the one hand people are rightly dissatisfied with the instruction which has been offered them in the name of enlightenment, and on the other they want to be left in peace, for they are suffering from spiritual fatigue. But surely it must be possible to convert the malcontents by explaining to them the true nature of enlightenment, and to put heart into the weary.

The men of to-day are weary indeed; and so they were before the war; they are both weary and resigned. They do not understand the world; and accordingly they no longer wish to understand it, and indeed they imagine that they get some pleasure from this incomprehension.

Men expatiate in the romantic and in the irrational. They do not ask after the meaning of these terms, or after that of their opposites. Rather they grow intoxicated in their ignorance, which they allege to be inevitable; for men have not only become resigned, but also intellectually slothful. They have neglected to train the will to think, and they have ended by becoming incapable of thought.

I

FALSE ENLIGHTENMENT AND GENUINE ENLIGHTENMENT

We will begin the detailed discussion by explaining that which may aptly be called false enlightenment: we will show the true nature of that which calls itself enlightenment but is not. It is dangerous because it can lead those who are convinced of the results to which it leads them unconsciously to commit non-good actions, while on the other hand it is apt to repel persons of a profounder nature, and lead those of them who lack the strength to conquer themselves into the misty regions of a resigned romanticism.

False enlightenment has two fundamental errors.

The first is that which holds that natural events are at bottom wholly mechanical, lacking order and plan. Conscious life is no more than a secondary epiphenomenon of the mechanism of nature.

The second is to the effect that all human actions are due to selfish impulses, and aim exclusively at the advantage of the agent. History is controlled solely by economic factors.

The first of these fundamental errors is, of course, a legacy of the xvIIIth Century; the second arose in the xIxth Century. Both are called materialism, although their meanings are not the same. Here, curiously enough, epistemological considerations are not practically of great importance; for even if mechanism is no more than the appearance of something which is unknown in itself, it still remains a mere aggregate and devoid of plan. This is the essential fact in this connection. It may also be mentioned that the enlightenment of the xvIIIth Century was free at least from the error of ethical-economical materialism. Early in the xIxth Century the two errors entered as allies upon their world-wide crusade of destruction.

The school of irrationalism and romanticism is right to protest against this form of enlightenment; for its principles are false, and are wrong upon matters of fact. But perhaps it is possible nevertheless that there should exist a genuine and satisfactory rational enlightenment.

We will begin by stating why the two principles are wrong.

The assertion that mechanism alone governs nature is wrong because it is possible to demonstrate by detailed analysis of biological facts that vital phenomena will not fit into the concept of mechanism—that is, into the doctrine that the whole of the empirical world can be explained by the reciprocal relation subsisting between

N

ultimate parts, whether we give to these the name of atoms, electrons, or quanta of energy. This also destroys the theory of the parallelism between the elements of mechanism and of the soul. It is simply not true that every future state of the universe can be foretold if at any given moment the position and velocity of the ultimate material elements are known, together with the elementary law which covers their interrelatedness and is laid down in the differential equations of physics.

Next, the theory that egoism, whether personal or economic, is the sole driving force in human activity (which includes what is called history) is wrong because it is possible to demonstrate immediately that there are other driving forces—namely, those which are of a moral or of an altruistic nature, although it is true that sometimes they take a curious form, as, for example, in the so-called holy wars (p. 152).

The old enlightenment, then, was no true and complete enlightenment: it did not give a full account of the nature of the world. We do not wish to detract from its merits. It has freed us from many errors: from the theory that the earth is the centre of the universe, that man is essentially different in nature from the animal creation, and that kings are of divinely ordained origin, to say nothing of the far more obvious errors of theological dogma. On the other hand, it wholly failed to see a great many facts and problems which form part of the empirical world.

2

GENUINE ENLIGHTENMENT

We must now ask what facts and questions a complete enlightenment should comprehend within its vision.

First of all, it must be a complete phenomenology of all that is an object of consciousness—that is, it must tell us definitely what clearly apprehended and significant entities can be the property of the conscious ego. Here, too, and at the very beginning, we lay the foundation of a complete psychology, as opposed to the inadequate theory of association of the old school of enlightenment. The peculiarity of our theory is that in it the concept of significance for an apprehending subject has a place among the first elements.[1] This, too, is the place of the roots of ethics: they consist in the demonstration that, when we apprehend of a thing that *it ought to be*, this intuition is a conscious and original phenomenon.

The most important of all things, however, which the critical phenomenology teaches us is that it is absolutely necessary to render a strict account in all intellectual matters whatsoever. Nothing must be allowed the right to exist save that which, to use Descartes' expression, is apprehended clearly and distinctly, or, as we may say, *definitively*. Knowledge and hypothetical assumption are two different things. This is a primary fact, and must be held fast for good, even in the practical sense. In this sense it is the foundation of tolerance in all matters of

[1] Cp. my *Grundproblem der Psychologie*, 1926.

mere assumption—that is to say, in regard to all those matters where no *definitive* knowledge is possible. Among these, as we know, are almost all particular ethical questions. Among ethical we also count political questions.

Next comes enlightenment about the concept of nature, and about empirical actuality in general. Given the nature of the concept of empirical actuality, what can exist potentially, and of this class, what actually does exist?

I consider that the question about the potentially existent is particularly important; about that which very well might be, although we are not, or are *not yet*, acquainted with it. This preserves us from a dogmatism like the pan-mechanism of the old enlightenment. Here the theory of causality is of particular importance. It teaches us that besides the mechanistic form of causality no less than three other forms of causality could subsist in nature,[1] only one of which has been demonstrated as being fulfilled empirically hitherto—that is, as actually subsisting, namely, vital causality, or causality which operates upon a totality. Why should one form of contemplation, that which begins from the parts of a composite structure, be called rational? Rather it is the concept of the totality, or that of order, which is the foundation of knowledge and of the desire for knowledge; and of all concepts is the most easily understood.

Next in the course of Enlightenment there follow scrupulous considerations about the possible existence

[1] Driesch, *Ordnungslehre*. Second edition, 1923, pp. 197 *sqq.*

of the objects of the theory of the supra-personal. Here the content of ethical intuition is employed, both as an epistemological and as a practical entity. On the theoretical side my *Wirklichkeitslehre*, and on the practical side the present work, attempts an effort in this direction; the intention of these books is as serious as, no doubt, the performance is imperfect.

The object of this discussion might also be called the theory of significance.[1] By significance we mean the significance of the world as a totality, or more particularly that of history: we mean that ultimate totality which is to be attained or realized by its temporal evolution.

The person upon whom the work of enlightenment is being undertaken must be convincingly impressed with the fact that we cannot here go beyond the consideration of possibilities. What is the goal of the development of life or of history? We do not and we cannot know; and we know precisely that we cannot know. This latter fact is demonstrable and forms part of Enlightenment.

Here hypotheses are permissible. All that is requisite is that they shall be methodical; and the first principle of method is that *entia*—that is, new and *essential* characteristics of reality—must not be posited *praeter necessitatem*, that is, unless they are demanded absolutely. This is an

[1] The word "significance" might also stand for the meaning of a concept, and of the word by which it is denoted. The word "relation" and the meaning which is denoted by it have a significance which, in this instance, cannot be defined. This meaning of the word "significance" must of course be carefully distinguished from that which it has in the text.

old doctrine, approved and formulated already by the Schoolmen. *Entia*, then, may be posited only when without them understanding cannot bring order into the facts which it attempts to apprehend.

Here we meet the problem of the single state and of the many individual states. We are taught that the power to form states is an essential trait which is part of the very nature of man, who is a ζῶον πολιτικόν, but that the historical rise and sequence of individual states is contingent, or, to express it for once in the language of theology, that the particular form in which they did in fact manifest themselves was not part of the divine will. Hence follows the theory that ethical responsibility exists unrestrictedly only towards man in general: responsibility towards the individual state exists only in so far it is pure and good *qua* state, and not as an end in itself, or for its own sake.

The postulate is this: "Be a citizen of the state in the best and noblest manner which lies in you, but do not comply with those aspects of the state which you intuit to be non-good; rather strive to remove them, without, however, using force."

Thus, in the field of the supra-personal, clear ethical intuition everywhere enters expressly into the discussion, which for its part is reflective and theoretical. This book is an example.

This, then, would also be the place at which to effect enlightenment about "honour", "glory", and kindred themes; among other errors that one might be removed which leads its victims to think that warlike glory is true glory, while it is true only that in war as in every other disaster the glory of self-sacrifice can exist.[1]

The most important task will always be to set out with complete lucidity the fundamental rules of the good and the bad, and more especially of the latter. There is no need to urge men to love their country; they will do so unasked. A certain degree of respect for the state, too, is generally found, although mostly in rather modest dimensions; and all that is needed is to strengthen it morally. But egoism too exists. This trait is particularly dangerous; and it should be combated with the utmost diligence wherever it hides behind a mask of collective egoism. Often this mask remains unseen, like that of national Jingoistic patriotism, and sometimes it even calls itself holy. Here Enlightenment has the right to use irony in order to be effective: for example, it might treat this kind of patriotism as being in a manner a characteristic of the aboriginal "native". The general rule will be to work consciously and in the spirit of true enlightenment towards the supra-national, for nationalism exists without external aid—generally in an intensive form.

[1] Scheler once argued in favour of war that it produces communities bound together by love. I do not know if he still thinks so. These communities of "love" turned out a rather doubtful proposition. But quite apart from this we would gladly go without such a community, even an ideal one, if it must owe its existence to the greatest sin of all—killing.

3
RATIONALISM

Finally Enlightenment treats of the limits of possible knowledge in general, and not of the limits which it has in regard to "meaning". Its function is to trace these limits as clearly as possible, without indulging in fine feelings or sentimentality, and without plunging into the depths which lie behind those emotions. Nothing is permitted here beyond cautious suppositions. The doctrine that there are limits here—that is, that there is something that is beyond the reach of knowledge—is itself a piece of knowledge. In other words, the theory of the existence of the irrational is itself in this sense rational.

Here, however, irrational merely means that which is beyond the scope of knowledge. Accordingly it may be equivalent to supra-rational, and need never mean anti-rational.

After all, there is not the slightest semblance of a reason for assuming that the highest reality is anti-rational. We might even go so far as to say that it is extremely improbable that the supreme cause is anti-rational, if we consider that reason, or *ratio*, does after all exist. Reason is the capacity of apprehending sensuously and without contradiction, and surely its origin resides in the highest cause: where else should be its origin? It is inconceivable that the highest should have created an instrument turned against itself.

To assume that the highest cause is anti-rational is the worst thinkable example of the process of positing an *ens praeter necessitatem*. We cannot here concern ourselves with vague romantic mystics. It is much to be desired that an end were made of romanticism; the world would be the better for it.

Accordingly *irrational* must simply mean, beyond the knowledge which we have as men. In this sense the irrational is due in the first place to the limitations of our senses and our understanding. It is probably the case that *all* that is real does not exist for us in the shape of a datum: all that is real is very far from "appearing" to us, whether in an intuitable or in a non-intuitable form. Phenomenally we intuit no more than fragments of reality, and our understanding of them is very inadequate. After all, there is nothing so very remarkable in this, nor is it any proof of anti-rationality.

Next, the irrational element has its origin in the fact that the world is saturated by contingency, and hence is dualistic. It is the nature of contingency that it is beyond the reach of knowledge: if we call a thing contingent this means that we do not comprehend it. Already Aristotle saw this. Evidently that which here causes facts to elude knowledge is something different from the fragmentariness of data. We cannot lay hold of contingency because of its vast and disordered multiplicity, and perhaps also in the last analysis it is indifferent: all that is necessary is to know once for all that it does exist and saturates everything. For this very reason history in almost all its ultimate details, and certainly in all its political details, is so indifferent to the world-view as a whole.

What do we mean by rational? I answer briefly: All that we can comprehend in its essence. But we can comprehend that only which is in some respects like ourselves. And we are creatures whose knowledge is directed upon totalities, and it follows from this that we can properly comprehend only totality and knowledge; while we can only apprehend in its order that which was the special darling of the old rationalism, namely, mechanism: comprehend it we cannot; unless, indeed, as some do, we refer the forces of matter to something spiritual within reality; and for this there is no valid ground. But we do really comprehend everything that has anything to do with knowledge, and consequently we have a better comprehension of telepathy and even of prophecy than, for example, of impulse, although we do not wholly comprehend them, unless we are ourselves paranormal. Thus even parapsychology, to say nothing of the theory of the subconscious, is to a certain extent rational.

We are human beings, and as such we cannot, of course, wholly comprehend why the world is as it is; at best we can surmise by faith, in a manner which resembles the processes of comprehension.

But in spite of this it thus appears that the scope of genuine Enlightenment is not inconsiderable.

4
"REALPOLITIK"

A man who is equipped with this kind of Enlightenment, and has not resolved to practise any kind of asceticism, but rather to act, will be free from every kind of conventional prejudice and limitation. He will be a strict judge of himself, but tolerant in his judgment of others.

As regards politics, he will, in the strictest sense of the term, pursue *Realpolitik*—that is to say, he will never aim at anything that is empirically impossible. But for him the ethical side of human nature, or action founded upon rational ethical intuition, will be a real factor, and not the fact alone that man is a being governed by impulses, having a place in a zoological system. And at the same time he will hold that he has knowledge of true reality when he understands the great fact that all men are of the same spiritual nature.

"You ought because you can": this is a rule which expresses this double truth, and he will respect it highly, and far more than the converse.

The consequences will be very beneficial for all, and not for the state only to which our politician happens to belong.

The religious wars ceased when men began to know their own ignorance—that is, when they knew that all the dogmas of the Church are tenets of faith which cannot be demonstrated, and are all equally valid and invalid, so that it is as ridiculous as it is unethical to force one's own faith upon another. Similarly political wars will cease when it is understood that no one people is better than another by nature, so that this, an "ideal", reason for waging war vanishes; and when, further, it is realized that it is possible to reach any understanding in all, even in economic, matters, and that an excuse can be found for killing, only in the rarest circumstances, which nowadays are never realized in practice.

The name of patriotism, properly understood, is a noble name: in our days a bastard patriotism, unworthy of that appellation, has frequently played the sorry part which in former ages was played by religious feelings distorted by sectarian zeal. These still remain to be discussed. Here ignorance of the real facts—an ignorance about human ignorance—was the very source of unethical action.

I am inclined to describe genuine Enlightenment as an education towards rationalism, by which, of course, I mean genuine rationalism. This rationalism apprehends the essential forms of the world in their totality, and in doing so apprehends its own limits.

In our days the word "rationalism" has achieved an evil odour, as also has "Enlightenment". There is no justification for this: the reason in each instance is too narrow a limitation of the subject-matter. With regard to rationalism as such, and apart from its service in the theory of Enlightenment, it must be remembered that rationalism is the theory of *all* the essential types, and not only of the mechanical ones. We cannot *completely* understand any of them, and the mechanical least of all. In no case do we understand why that is an essential type which happens to be one, and equally we fail to understand why some of the potential essential types exist empirically, while others do not. But we do understand what is really significant in all the essential types, and we understand best of all the non-mechanical element in them—the element of totality.

We therefore deliberately adopt the programme of rationalism and enlightenment.

5
THE EFFECTS OF RATIONAL ENLIGHTENMENT

It may be asked what influence Enlightenment can have upon action, if there is no such thing as freedom, or indeterminism, even if by freedom we mean no more than that we have the power to assent to or dissent from contents of will, the occurrence of which is determined, so that we are free only to admit (or exclude) the *realization* of contents of will. We have already stated that we can neither demonstrate nor refute the existence of such a freedom (pp. 23 *sqq.*), so that the possibility remains that the ego is wholly inactive and a mere recipient entity. In that case its recipient passivity would not be modified by that slight degree of freedom which consists in the power to admit or exclude contents of will.

We have already demonstrated that Ethics as a system can exist even if the facts are such. But the question is,

Can it in that case influence action in any manner; can it make men better?

The answer is, that that is not the immediate aim of Ethics. We must never forget, and must rather once more assert, that the first aim of ethics is merely to apprehend clearly what must be the nature of the will and action of souls, both of my own and of those of others, in order that I shall be able to say of them, "It ought to be so". Here there is no question of freedom or the reverse. The concept of "ought" is analysed, and the guidance of empirical facts is followed in order to pursue it into all its details: that is all. It is true, of course, that we are speaking of an activity of the soul when, for example, it is said that it would be good if this activity were turned upon the making of laws, but only of certain laws and not of too many, in order to avoid rigidity. We are not here investigating whether these laws might also not be made, whence we might conclude whether they owe their origin to a free will or not. The discussion is turned wholly upon objects: in the given object it intuits the form of the *ought* in various modifications.

Now, however, we come to a very significant matter, which gives a meaning to the results of ethical intuition even if we take up a deterministic standpoint. Where it is the case that something ought to be, and we behold its realization, then this event is accompanied by pleasure, and all that I wish for, or desire to see, is that which will bring about that which ought to be. And I know as a matter of experience that Enlightenment by contemplation about that which ought to be does in fact bring about the will to the good and the realization of the good. It does so both in my soul, when I discover and teach that which ought to be, and in the souls of the others whom I instruct. This may or may not be a part of the pre-determined plan: I cannot tell. It may be that my intuition and my teaching and the reaction of my own soul and of those of others are part of a plan, and that all these events together are the unfolding of one drama. It does not matter. It is, at any rate, *as though* my teaching, based upon contemplation, did act upon myself (my soul) and upon others; and in this sense ethics in spite of everything can become a useful system of rules. And having intuited all this, I also intuit the obligation to teach others in order that my doctrine shall be applied to myself and others, and thus shall become fruitful; I may and I must say: "Here stand I, I cannot otherwise, God help me."

To this must be added new discoveries of science, which have given us new powers, and what might almost be called a new technique, for exerting influence upon my own soul and those of others.

The doctrine of auto-suggestion in the state of relaxation has latterly become the property of science.[1] Its contents have been known for many years under a religious-metaphysical shape both to Indians and to various Christian sects, to the one under the name of doctrines of Yoga, and to the other as Christian Science.

[1] Cp. Baudouin, *Suggestion et Autosuggestion*.

Intellectually and morally, and even physically, I as psycho-physical person can become better; I can thus improve myself, not indeed if I expressly will to become better, but if I impress the thought of future improvement, so to speak, into the unconscious in a semi-hypnotic state.

It is the duty of those who have recognized this truth to apply it. It would be false pride to struggle against it on the ground that it involves a kind of abdication of the conscious ego in favour of the unconscious soul, although of course the will to the auto-suggestive process is always conscious. (Cp. *Grundproblem der Psychologie*, p. 217.)

For the rest, this method has always been applied unconsciously by those who wished to enforce their will—a will which generally was directed upon evil. This is the origin of almost all opinions and ideals of the day.

The task is consciously to allow the unconscious to rule, but to restrict its action to the service of what has been intuited to be definitive—that is, good.

It is impossible even to imagine to what a pitch of perfection this method might carry us, since Freud and Coué have succeeded in making the subconscious the instrument of conscious volition, and hence of *ratio*. For education there is no instrument more powerful than this. We now know the good and the bad sides of the dynamics of the subconscious, and it lies in our power to give play to either of them. The next move lies with the professional educators; and it is to be hoped that they will avail themselves of this opportunity. (Cp. pp. 131 *sqq*.)[1]

I am well aware that there are many and popular catchwords which oppose this view. It is said with regret that we have lost our sureness of instinct, that we have lost touch with life, and that Intellect has killed life. Domination ought to belong to the Impulses, the subconscious, and to the "It".

Nobody can attach a higher value to the investigation of the subconscious than myself, if only on the score of the enormous contribution which it makes to knowledge. Practically, and more particularly from the ethical point of view, its investigation is of such great importance because the intellect now possesses the necessary knowledge which enables it to make use of these investigations to control the subconscious, so that its absolute domination is ended. It was precisely this that was needed; for although it may be the case that the "It" has been the source of some good, it is certain that it was the source of far more evil. We might go so far as to assert that the supreme cause created the maligned intellect in order to master Impulses and the Subconscious, both of which were dangerous. We must repeat again and again that the intellect itself has its origins in that common source. What ought to be brought about is precisely this, that the

[1] We have intentionally said little of Psychical Research in this work, for that science belongs to the future, and as yet the theory of it is incomplete. It is my conviction that it is destined some day to bring about a fundamental change in our entire world-view. The result will be a profound transformation of the ethical life of the whole of mankind towards the better.

much praised "Approach to Life" is subjected to ethical rule, and that all that does not stand the test of ethics, of which there is a great deal, shall be overcome. This is the task of intellect according to its essence; and this is none the less true if hitherto it has been very ill-fulfilled, and even if intellect, as we cannot deny, often strayed from the path. But in spite of this we once more praise genuine Enlightenment, and the people which deliberately makes it its guide.

6

OBSTACLES AND HOW THEY ARE OVERCOME

The romantic modern tendency against Enlightenment was described above as spiritual sloth—as the surrender of conscious weakness in the face of great difficulties. I should now like to say something about another form of sloth.

The form of sloth with which I dealt above was intellectual: it was a shirking of hard thought. A man fails to make any progress in thought; he gives it up, and —it does not here matter whether he was free to do so or not—he takes refuge in a belief in the supra-rational, and even in the anti-rational.

Here, however, we are speaking of what may be called a form of practical sloth; it is found chiefly in the field of practical politics. The friends of non-rationality and of romanticism in intellectual matters have their counterpart in the practical sphere in the shape of "Conservatives".

What both aim at is to be left in peace; the one group want peace from their own thoughts and the other from external events. So they proceed to say that a civilization cannot be made, that it is an organic growth, and that no further trouble need be taken. "For heaven's sake no change" is the cry.

I must admit that the conscious ego cannot bring about any change, the reason being that the ego is not an active entity; this is my own doctrine, and I insist upon it with the utmost emphasis. But *souls* are capable of effective action, and the conscious experience of volition is the evident proof that they are so.

At bottom, then, the man who teaches the doctrine of organic growth would seem to mean that the soul is to effect as little as possible. The action of the soul must not proceed by leaps.

Here the man who follows the genuine method of Enlightenment has the right to ask *why* not. Even in conservative politics something is done; even there occasional changes take place in the laws, and even in the constitution; only they are generally rather insignificant.

One fails to see why such changes should not be of the greatest scope once the eyes have been opened by Enlightenment, and have seen that the proposed changes are good. A change is a change whether it is great or little, and even a Conservative does not wish to live quite without change.

It is true that great changes can be unpleasant: some

consider them inadequate, and others excessive; and they are apt to lead to conflict of opinions if to nothing worse; for those where intuition is absolutely true and clear are few and far between.

In spite of all this, ethics demands that the duly considered attempt be made to realize uncompromisingly that which Enlightenment has shown to be good. The teacher who brings Enlightenment must, of course, proceed with prudence and moderation. Thus, as was already said at a previous place, no reasonable person will give the vote to the whole population—including those who cannot write or read—in a state which hitherto did not possess a universal vote, although he will take care that the population learns to write and read as soon as possible: and to this extent and to this extent alone he will urge a gradual change, such as the facts demand. But what of the transition from monarchy to republic? We know that it is a political system which has no ethical justification, and where it is newly instituted confers no dignity even for the monarch. Surely such a transition cannot be gradual, for a king who is only a fraction of a king is unthinkable. And how are we to imagine a gradual transition from slavery to be brought about? Are slave-owners to be restricted to three slaves at first, and to no more? It seems to me that once it is seen [1] that slavery ought not to be it must be abolished

[1] In the days when war was supposed to be a divine judgment this was not understood by either side: even those who were carried into slavery thought that their fate was just. But a day came when they no longer thought so. Ethically this settled the question.

altogether. And as a matter of history it has been abolished in this form.

And how is war to be abolished gradually? We have already demonstrated the ethical dangers which are implied in indulging in war "just for one last time".

For the rest, the words "organic growth" do not even express what the Conservatives mean them to express; and if they knew the meaning of organic growth they would not in all probability make use of this figure. I propose to employ this figure against them, with results which probably will surprise them not a little.

We are, then, dealing with organic development for the purpose of our metaphor, and not with mere growth in the narrower sense. In mere growth nothing new arises, and all that happens is that the parts which are already in existence grow bigger. Now even the Conservatives do not desire to see nothing new whatever in the state.

Now embryology does proceed quite expressly by means of leaps. From one homogeneous totality of cells one or more cells separate *suddenly*, and these constitute the germ of a new organ which up to this point did not exist at all. In this way the process continues, and always does so by leaps, until the so-called process of differentiation is completed. After this point growth consists simply in an increase in size.

On the other hand, if it is desired for purposes of analogy to make use of phylogeny, the laws of which science are almost wholly unknown, then it must be stated that no reasonable person nowadays denies that it is extremely probable that phylogenetic leaps occur at certain decisive points in the history of living entities. Small leaps occur only at the points where so-called mutations arise within a species; and even these small leaps are not equivalent to continuous variation; and the results of continuous variation are not inherited.

We must, then, leave those who defend organic growth in politics to themselves and to their own sluggishness. Let us join practical to intellectual courage. It goes without saying that this action must take place with the greatest prudence, self-examination, and honesty. But once contemplative Enlightenment has found that a course of action is good, then it must also be preached. We know as a matter of historical fact that if a man preaches much he will achieve something, but if he preaches little and with hesitation, he will achieve nothing at all. For there are many obstacles, partly because the masses are lazy, and partly because a one-sided and headstrong Enlightenment has made them "radical".

It is true that social and political life *ought* to be rationalized by means of a thorough Enlightenment—that is, it ought to be moulded in accordance with reason; but it must be clearly understood that this implies a complete Enlightenment—that is to say, an Enlightenment which makes use of everything that has been intuited to be definitive; and this includes every apprehension of a totality, and everything that is apprehended in a cognitive-instinctive manner. There is no other way in which the good can find expression in the life of the state. But everything that is apprehended to be good is a part of Enlightenment; and it is one of the factors of *Realpolitik* that men are good, at least in one of their spiritual aspects, since they would like to realize the good if they could.

Those good old times of which men are so fond of speaking were in reality far from good; and those who to-day praise the civilization of Greece and of Weimar above everything forget how few were those who had a share in these civilizations, and how base was the position of those who were excluded from them. A less perfect civilization of which all can partake is more valuable, even from the ethical point of view; and the time will come when such a civilization provides the foundation for a highest form of civilization without a flaw. It is to be feared, however, that this will not take place in Europe in the immediate future.

Certainly it is foolish to speak ill of all that is old merely because it is old; but it is far more foolish to praise it for that reason. Some old institutions are good, but unfortunately they are few. Essentially, therefore, we must look forward, and it is more important that we shall be worthy of our descendants than of our ancestors. Tradition has become the curse of Europe.

In the first instance, of course, it will be the task of the schools to bring these ethical postulates nearer to realization. It is the function of the school to educate the young generation—that is, to *lead it up* into an ethical frame of mind. The young person is to be educated: the education of the teacher must have been perfected.

Most of the observations which I have to make about the question of education have already been made at a former place (pp. 130 *sqq.*), and all that I wish to add here is the following. The great task of the schools is to educate the young to reach a frame of mind of true rationality with the help of teachers who have been rationally educated. And true rationality means to look facts in the face as they are—both the facts of nature and ethical facts. We are already acquainted with the proposition that we can act only in so far as we know the laws of the real. This requires that far more *real* knowledge shall be imparted in the schools than to-day—that is, essential and exact psychology, sociology, and science. At present our schools are far too vaguely literary and historical— too idealistic in the hollow sense of the term. We look far too much into the past, and too little into the future. We intoxicate ourselves with the pathos of Schiller, but we forget the words of the greater man: those words which tell us how reason becomes unreason, and how the good turns into a plague; and we forget the terrible truth of the final: "An heir—a man accursed." History must, of course, be taught, but it must not be taught in order that the changes in human nature shall be known, for, as we have seen, such changes do not exist. The teaching of history should point to the great examples which exist to prove that in the course of centuries an improvement has taken place in human powers of understanding, and that in every respect, both intellectually and morally, so that an increase in understanding is possible for the future too.

Education must not turn out heirs of the past, but future fathers and mothers, whose function it will be to look with a clear glance into the future, full of knowledge and ethical intuition. Then alone our past history will cease to be for us a cause of suffering.

IV

RELIGION AS THE AIM OF ENLIGHTENMENT

RELIGIOUS Enlightenment is the highest form of Enlightenment, and I propose to conclude this work by discussing it and setting it up as the goal of endeavour.

The fact is that enlightenment and religion are so far from being incompatible that the religious state can be described as the last goal of all true Enlightenment. We need not hesitate to describe this ultimate aim of Enlightenment by the words of that old thinker who spoke of *amor intellectualis dei*: for this is our approximate meaning.

I

THE RELIGIOUS STATE, RELIGION, AND METAPHYSICS

The religious state is a feeling, and like every feeling it is the conscious expression of a state of the unconscious soul. Now every feeling has an object for kernel: we are afraid *of something*, we hope *for something*, and we are pleased *about something*. Now the religious state is a feeling of surrender and of joyful repose in the consciousness of perfect security in the power of another. Dependence must not be the sole characteristic; the feelings of a slave towards his master were certainly no religious feelings. The primitives have fear before their god and nothing more, and their religious feelings are incomplete and admit of improvement.

Thus all religious feelings have an intellectual kernel, a kernel of knowledge. This kernel may be apprehended vaguely, or clearly and distinctly. Religious feelings are the more perfect, the more clearly and distinctly the kernel of knowledge is apprehended upon which they are based. Such knowledge is given by Enlightenment. In this sense Buddhism is the most perfect religion. If we consider the religious state from its emotional aspect, its kernel is found to be Religion or religious belief; apart from this state, it is a metaphysical assumption having subjectively a high degree of probability.

Belief, or metaphysical assumption, has for its sphere the doctrine of the totality and the evolution of the world. It is supposed throughout that I, as psycho-physical person, am initiated into this totality and evolution.

Now it is true that all knowledge of supra-personal things is hypothetical, and it can even be demonstrated that it follows from the nature of man that it cannot be other. Nevertheless it is possible to formulate certain assertions which have some degree of probability, to the effect that in fact I do possess an initiation into the evolution of the totality. The totality, and the evolution which is predicated of it, is not, of course, co-extensive with the earth, and the goal, or the final totality which is reached in the course of evolution, is not a state of earthly perfection, as, for example, a "socially" perfect state would be.

The most essential foundation for this doctrine consists in the fact that ethical subjects capable of intuition do exist. But there are other foundations as well.

The subject who possesses ultimate metaphysical intuition also possesses all particular metaphysical knowledge, for the latter is included in the former. But a man who has ultimate metaphysical insight in the form of the religious state has at the same time an attitude towards the world which is of a volitional nature, and brings his soul nearer to goodness and draws it away from badness, if it does not actually make it perfect. As for the nature of this ultimate insight, I consider that it changes automatically into the religious state, and that the feelings which accompany it *qua* insight carry the religious note.

Empirically it is the case that the religious man is made better in this manner: he bears a charm, which, although it will not preserve him against temptations or against an occasional fall, will help him in his fight with temptations and the powers that try to bring him down.

The religious man is in an emotional state, that of religious emotion, which consists of a calm joy based upon perfect Enlightenment. It is entirely desirable that he shall have *this* emotion, for it is the source of all good. At the same time it is the function of this *amor intellectualis* to cast out all those emotions which are a part of human frailty and have their origin in the egoistic impulses. These are the source of almost all evil, and more especially of all violent intentions, whether of a personal or of a collective nature. A man who, inspired by this emotion, takes up his stand within the totality, sees from that vantage-point what is good and what is bad in the individuals, and gains power to help the good and to stamp out the bad within himself.

Logically ethical intuition comes first, and metaphysics takes the second place, for the concepts of the real in general and of the supra-personal totality, and of evolution in particular, are employed in order to render intelligible the existence of "ethical intuition".

Metaphysically, however, that which is posited metaphysically (which includes the religious kernel of knowledge) is taken as the foundation of the ethical concepts. Without this foundation the ethical concepts are in the air, and it was precisely for this reason that the metaphysical postulates were used in order to explain ethical intuition.

This is the philosophical statement of the matter. In ordinary life, however, without intending it, we always speak metaphysically. Thus for everyday and unsophisticated life metaphysics is the theoretical and religion the practical foundation of everything. Now at this point it may be urged that ethical rules are not really binding upon the intellect, however immediately and impressively they may be given, unless they have a metaphysical or religious basis, since, without it, they may be illusory. Further, in order that ethical rules shall be completely binding upon the individual, it seems as though in practice there must always be a certain belief in immortality and in genuine freedom. This belief would be a particular form of metaphysics, in which the belief in immortality is more closely connected with the concept of guilt than with that of reward. Accordingly, a "primacy" of the ethical rule can exist only for the philosopher and never for the ordinary man, and even the philosopher abandons this primacy, and demands an ultimate reason for the ethical rule. Perhaps he even indulges in some slight belief in freedom, and still more in immortality.

Even in our day men are not quite clear about these facts. Nevertheless they exist, and it is inevitable that they should exist. It is a fact that for those who absolutely deny immortality all things are at bottom ethically indifferent. Such men will as a rule be atheists and materialists, or at any rate they will hold mechanistic beliefs. Human nature is so constituted that even these beliefs will not suffice to blind those who hold them to ethical intuition, or deafen them to the voice of conscience (and this fact alone constitutes the so-called primacy of practical reason). But they cannot be truly binding. If a man has such beliefs he is rather bound to tell himself that nature has committed upon him a sort of fraud and deception in order to preserve the race or the species; and ethics here cannot but turn into an instinct for the preservation of the species, and no more. But we may ask how far he is concerned with the species, and how far the species is concerned with itself, if life is nothing more than a rather complicated kind of mechanics, and life and spirit are no more than an "epiphenomenon".

In fact, a man who denies immortality cannot consistently be a consciously ethical person, and if in practice he generally is an ethical being, this fortunate fact is due to his theoretical inconsistency.

The case is different for those who believe in immortality. For them conscience is no illusion, and its essence is to be part of the very essence of the world. Now it would not be a matter of great importance if immortality were believed in merely in order that ethical intuition should become essential and important. But such concepts as the real, the supra-personal, and immortality occur in other regions besides that of ethics, and accordingly there is a certain sense (although not the strict sense) in which they may be spoken of as *causae verae*; and this is sufficient to explain the existence of ethics, and to justify its rules. Perhaps a future parapsychology will some day transform them into genuine *causae verae*.

It is certainly possible, then, for a materialistic philosopher to be ethically inspired as a man; but at bottom such a state would be philosophically inconsistent. A true justification for ethical intuition can be based on one foundation only, namely, a metaphysics of spirit which in some form implies immortality.

2

RATIONAL EMOTIONS

We described the religious state as a feeling, and we even went so far as to praise the *amor intellectualis*, which is an emotion; and yet at the beginning of this work (p. 47) we spoke of the danger involved in an uncritical acceptance of anything emotional, and emphasized the importance of effecting a clear distinction between genuinely cognitive feelings and feelings which are merely habitual. It looks as though there were some inconsistency here.

The inconsistency can be resolved if we carefully analyse the *amor intellectualis*, treating it as an emotion. The expression means love based upon knowledge; it thus denotes an emotion to which *ratio* has granted its approval. The emotion itself is of great practical importance because, like every other emotion, it has the power to direct the will. At the same time it works towards the good because justification precedes it, or, if we prefer to put it that way, goes hand in hand with it.

Feelings, and especially feelings in their strongest form, namely emotions, are practically of great importance in influencing the will, and precisely for this reason their justification must be examined with particular exactness, unless ethical harm is to result. We know already that they often are not original cognitive data, nor the results of clear and specialized knowledge, but are the products of habit and suggestion. Such are a great many emotions which are called patriotic, and in fact are chauvinistic, which at school were implanted into the pupils by teachers who were perhaps honest subjectively, but lacked Enlightenment. The result is that they are firmly fixed in the mind and determine the will, a source of harm to the country and to mankind in general.

Thus, while we accord the highest praise to the religious feeling as *amor intellectualis*, we urge at the same time the greatest caution in trusting this feeling. Vague feelings are a very grave danger for ethics, and it is better deliberately to free the will from the influence of all feeling whatsoever, and to take up a perfectly unmoved attitude, than to surrender uncritically to every emotion, feeling, or impulse, or whatever else we may choose to call it.

No man has the right to follow his feelings for any length of time without consciously testing them, unless his intellectual conscience has given its approval. Even when this has been granted, it is essential, as we have already stated (p. 224), that a fresh test be made from time to time. For man is a being that is subject to error and to selfishness, and it may have been the case that he did not see clearly, or even that selfishness prevented him unconsciously from seeing clearly, where he had the power to see.

Here, where we are dealing with the justification of feelings, we must take another matter into consideration which makes it exceedingly difficult correctly to judge their value in determining the will. It is possible that a lack of logical insight allows a feeling to appear to be justified "cognitively" when in fact it is not justified; and further, the feeling, the existence of which is not denied, can lead the soul astray, and present to consciousness alleged reasons which in fact are not reasons at all. To put it in popular language, we know perfectly well that our wishes often determine that which we

P

imagine ourselves to see; I would like a certain fact to be true, and the intellectual side of the soul becomes the obedient servant of this wish—*intellectus voluntatis ancilla*.

This danger is the greatest of all, and it is greater than the danger of error due to inadequate insight into all the facts of the case. The only safeguard against this danger consists in a very high measure of self-discipline. To begin with, we must assume that all our feelings are due to selfish impulses; we must first subject them to a rigorous examination; and not until this has been carried out shall we be able to say that one or the other of them has a cognitive justification. At the same time it is essential never to lose sight of the fact that every aspect of the case has not yet been completely understood. The process by which scientific theories are formed is somewhat similar, and for this reason scientists should have a peculiar capacity for an unbiased apprehension of ethical truth and falsehood. Unfortunately, events have proved that this is not the case.

In general, then, any worship of the feelings is dangerous. Any man who claims the right to follow his feelings for a certain way must have the power of exercising keen self-criticism preceded by careful examination; and those who have a talent for keen self-criticism are few and far between.

To-day we know only too well the harm that can be done by feeling, and which will be done if the wishes of some of its worshippers are fulfilled.

Once more, then, we would say that it would be better not to have any feelings at all, and in their place passionless contemplation: such a contemplation need not necessarily be directed upon other objects than utility, although of course it must apprehend clearly and must go down to ultimate principles, and must not be egoistic. This would be better than a feeling which could not be justified before the intellectual conscience, or *ratio*.

Certainly subjective honesty is a good thing, and a man who is subjectively honest deserves the respect even of his opponents. This kind of honesty is found among many worshippers of the feelings, especially in the sphere of politics. Nevertheless, all permissible means must be employed in order to prevent it from becoming objectively dangerous.

Kant says that the only thing that is wholly good is the good intention: but this is true only if the content of this intention can stand the test of reason. Consequently good intentions must be accompanied by an intellect which lies open to good and genuine Enlightenment, if real good is to result; otherwise the proverb of the "Good men, but bad musicians", will apply. Politics in particular is a kind of music which can become exceedingly dangerous if, in spite of the best intentions in the world, the performance is poor.

Of course we agree with Kant that good intentions as such are an essential condition of objective goodness. And, fortunately, those who suffer from moral insanity are not many.

It is the primitive man who abandons himself to his feelings, and civilization is the road from dim feelings to the clear consciousness of reason, which is far from despising the subconscious, but knows its limits, and makes use of it as a powerful force in its service. The politicians who deal in feelings will always wear, in the eyes of the true rationalist, something of the air of an "aborigine" in the special sense which belongs to this word.

One might even be tempted to say that the worship of the feelings is a relic of our animal nature. But we are men, and this means that *ratio*, or reason, in the profoundest sense of the word, has been given us in order that we shall make use of it, that is, in order that we shall consciously subordinate to it all that is of the nature of feeling or impulse, and all that is of the nature of the subconscious. Ethical clearness of vision is the highest apex of reason. We must let beasts be beasts: for ourselves, we must consciously be men.

It was necessary to say all this in order to justify the apparent contradiction between our praise of the religious emotion and our rejection of a worship of the feelings in general. I now proceed to examine the religious state as an emotion.

To be man means to apprehend laws, and having apprehended them, to force them into the service of the demands of ethics. This application of laws in the service of ethics is the highest kind of "technique", based upon genuine rationality.

To-day it is unhappily true to say that although the science which we possess has taken upon itself many of the coarser burdens of mankind, yet in spite of this it has done more harm than good. The terrible fruits which *ratio*, or spirit, has produced up to our days have been described with great power by Theodor Lessing.

It need not be so.[1] Already this has been widely perceived, and many communities, among them the Quakers, have placed science in the service of the good.

The highest science of all, however, is the science of mankind, used in the service of the good—a science which has been formulated by Freud, Coué, Baudouin, and (at an earlier period) by Myers. Here the laws of the soul stand in the service of the will, for every so-called process of suggestion is preceded by the resolve to enter upon it. As yet we are at the very beginnings. But I

[1] Lessing is often interpreted as meaning that the spirit in general is the source of all evil. I do not think that this correctly represents his view. What he means is the spirit which violently isolates itself from reality (or Life) and makes itself its antagonist—in short, egoistic spirit. He does not mean spirit which knows itself to be part of a totality. Thus he writes: "That which gives a meaning to a human life is not to ask in each instance, like common men, What do I need? but, Who needs me?" (*Untergang der Erde*, p. 456.) According to Lessing, what ails Europe is, "Not intellect or mechanism or rationalism, but rather the fact that it is not adapted to these human forces". (*Ibid.*) He strongly criticizes "vague adoration of the irrational", and goes on to say (*ibid.*, p. 460): "It is not spirit in general which is bringing about the destruction of the world, for it is spirit precisely which is the life of its life and the essence of its essence; the harm is done by spirit which has been forced from and has passed beyond its proper sphere, and which (in man) stands objectively opposed to the earth." Cp. also *Geschichte als Sinngebung usw.*, 1927, pp. 126 and 311: "I do not oppose pure spirit as the enemy of life—it is the very kernel of life; but the spirit which has been severed from the earth: the flame which has struck outward."

believe that a time will come when the science of mankind will have been perfected, a science which will be founded upon *ratio*, and will lead to the highest perfection of *ratio*. When that is reached, man will not "follow" his feelings or impulses; they will follow him in the service of the highest.

3
TRUE ENLIGHTENMENT AND RELIGION

What our time lacks is the religious spirit, and this lack is the cause of its many ills. Bare ethics of a neo-Kantian or neo-Protestant character are an insufficient substitute for the religious spirit. This much is obvious.

On the other hand we witness a striving after religion. Many men, however, still misguidedly base their hopes upon a false and narrow enlightenment, which, although it was right in removing a great many kinds of superstition, has proceeded to the error of treating as a superstition everything that is not of the nature of an aggregate and everything that is not mechanistic or associative. A man with a religious disposition who is involved in the error of false enlightenment is unhappy and to be pitied. He seeks, but in the narrow circle in which he is held he cannot find. Take, for example, an advocate of hylozoism, or, as he wrongly calls himself, Monist. He is deeply involved in the doctrines of false enlightenment, and at the same time he has profound moral intuition. Now, if he proceeded in a manner consistent with this erroneous premiss, then, as we already know, he ought to declare the whole of ethics to be an illusion without foundation; for the man who teaches that the world is an aggregate can have no real system of ethics in the proper and binding sense of the term. Now his original ethical intuition is in perpetual conflict with this alleged intellectural truth, whence result such curious doctrines as that of a "religious" feeling caused by the laws of the preservation of matter and of energy. Such a man is not aware that he simply did not pursue his thoughts to their logical conclusion, and that the enlightenment of which he was so proud was incomplete; for, while applying the process of enlightenment, he has forgotten that he himself exists as an ethical and thinking subject.

If a man confines himself to the region of true enlightenment, and contemplates all things while striving after perfection *sub specie aeternitatis*, then no other state is possible for him than one of calm love and of pity: he can neither hate nor judge others with bitter words. His pity will be free from pride or obtrusiveness, even if he feels that he has a mission; for he did not create for himself his knowledge, and even less his intelligent sympathy. These qualities are the gifts of that greatest and highest principle within which he is no more than a point; and this he knows.

He also knows that all that is earthly is no more than a parable, that is, that it is no more than a single image, dualistically distorted, of a prototype, which has its place in another world, which is its proper sphere according to its true essence.

But as it is, he is planted in the realm of earth as a knowing and ethical subject. All that surrounds him is, as we know, mere hypothesis. We also know that he can take up the ascetic attitude and renounce all that is earthly; and he can do so by the negation of action, or of life itself.

But if this negation does not take place, we know further that he *ought* to let his actions be guided solely by the will to act *well*. And in this resolve nothing is of such help and strengthening power as the spirit of religion. This is an empirical fact.

Accordingly, if the process of Enlightenment is undertaken, it should be carried to its extremest limit—that is, up to the justification of true religion. For it is possible to give an intellectual justification of religion with a good conscience.

Our Socialists are for the most part still in the toils of a false enlightenment, and the majority of them accordingly is hostile to religion and to metaphysics. They think that they are intellectually honest, and to this extent they *are* intellectually honest; but they are involved in error. This is precisely the place where true Enlightenment must begin to do its work. It must be inspired by love, and must be far removed from a spirit of contempt, mockery, or insult. If it is convincingly demonstrated that the teaching of the alleged Enlightenment is false, then all the alleged consequences of the "scientific result" of this Enlightenment will drop away automatically. Having achieved knowledge through pity, men will cease to hold the view that they have the right to enforce their social convictions at the point of the bayonet, still less that they ought to do so. It goes without saying that every suspicion of superior unction must be avoided here. And before a man has the right to teach that anything is a piece of true enlightenment he himself must be satisfied that it really is self-evident: this is the only criterion.

The nationalists of all the nations are idolaters. It is true that they worship a highest principle; but this supreme principle is the individual state which they treat as divine. It is irrelevant that they give to their god a Christian dress: he is none the less a national god. It would be more honest here to put old Wotan upon the throne once more; only Wagner's Wotan must not be selected, for he ends by becoming a Buddhist. ("One thing only I now desire—the end.")

Here, too, true Enlightenment must not despair. It would appear as though it had an easier task than it has when dealing with those who teach that the world is by nature an aggregate, and all that results thence; for here the idea of totality does already exist, although in a false disguise. But in fact its task is all the more difficult, for it is easier for a form of enlightenment to enforce itself if it brings with it an entirely new logical structure than if it is obliged first to remove the contents of an already existing framework; just as it is easier to learn good Spanish if that is the first romance language which is being attacked than if the learner can already speak Italian.

The task of Enlightenment is more difficult with the nationalists than with the masses who had been receiving a false enlightenment. The former generally belong to the educated classes; and, further, the position of things is such that, when genuine enlightenment takes place, the masses can retain most of their practical ideals, and all that happens is that they are recommended to apply them practically in another form, apart from the fact that a new set of reasons is advanced for their foundation. On the other hand, the educated classes witness the entire subversion of their own particular ideals. (We are not here thinking of such questions as that of loss of prestige or of caste or property, because these are selfish and unworthy.)

To resume once more the practical considerations, it is easier to exert intellectual and practical influence upon an "uneducated" Socialist in the sense of genuine enlightenment, leading up to the justification of religion, than it is to lead an "educated" nationalist up to genuine enlightenment, for the reason that it is easier to build where nothing has been built before than it is to pull down old buildings and then to begin anew; quite apart from the fact that in the second case selfish resistances of a practical nature have to be overcome.

But the teacher of genuine enlightenment sees no difficulties: he only has his goal in view.

4

RELIGIOUS DENOMINATIONS: THE CHURCH

Up to this point I have been speaking only of the religious spirit, and not at all of religious denominations or of the Church; it now remains simply to discuss whether in doing so I tacitly had in mind these historical institutions or not.

I did not have them in mind, and all that I had in mind was the religious spirit, of which I was speaking. This is the ultimate source of all moral action, and in my opinion, if war is rejected on principle, the reason is implicit in the religious spirit.

Church-doctrine is the teaching of religion in its dogmatic form; it does not offer a clear justification to reason, but is given as a "revelation". Where this form is lacking, there no Church can exist as a social institution; from whence it follows immediately that none of the "liberal" Protestant communities is a "Church".

All genuine Church-doctrines have a valid logical-metaphysical kernel; and this is true especially of the two doctrines which are most completely developed—the Roman Catholic Church and the religious doctrine of India. There is, of course, a certain kinship between the metaphysical kernels of these two systems, and in some respects they resemble neo-platonism.

Now, I do not urge that men *ought* to join a genuine Church—that is, a social institution having its foundation in dogma; and I do not urge it for the reason, first, that it is impossible to give advice in matters of dogma, and, secondly, that I consider all existing Church-doctrines to be dogmatic (the least dogmatic being the Hinayana Buddhism), and, finally, because I cannot make up my mind to accept any one of them, although, of course, it is impossible to demonstrate that they are "wrong".

But I am not opposed to any Church as such so long as its doctrines are not in conflict with what I apprehend to be metaphysical truth and the demands of ethics; and this is not the case with the Roman Catholic Church and the teachings of Buddha. These are the only two doctrines which teach that the spirit of man is one, and in this sense both of them are Christian in the original sense of the word. They exist for the benefit of all peoples; whereas a certain Protestant Church has introduced the concept of the State-Church and thus has cut itself off from the purest source of true doctrine, and has even opened the door to certain ways of thought which are wholly anti-Christian.

In matters of the Church, then, all men are free to act as they will. If they are satisfied by the true religious spirit as it is given them by a Church, then they should join an ecclesiastical community; if not, they should remain without.

It might be asked whether it might not be possible to found a new Church, since we may observe beginnings in that direction in the theosophical and the anthropo-sophical movements, and in the Salvation Army.

In my opinion a new Church is to-day an utter impossibility. My reason is that every Church has a "magical" aspect and is based upon the concept of "revelation", which is supposed to be a non-natural and historically unique source of knowledge; or upon the concept of the "priest", a man who has acquired his powers in a non-natural manner; or upon both. By non-natural I do not mean rare and abnormal powers, like those which are manifested in "psychical" phenomena, although it is possible that the concepts of "revelation" and of "priest" are originally due to the fact that phenomena of this kind became familiar to the congregation, since such phenomena necessarily would *seem* peculiarly mysterious, and, in fact, would always *be* so: they are so even to-day. What I mean by the words "magical" and "non-natural" is something which by its very essence is such that it cannot yield its secret to science. Such phenomena as "revelation" (for example, in the shape of speaking with tongues) and "priest" (for example, in the form of the thought-reader, or even of the prophet) can enter into the sphere of scientific investigation, and even of experiment: but as soon as this happens the true revelation and the true priest are lost for ever.

By the word "non-natural" as applied to *revelation* and to *priest* is meant the true miracle, which can be attributed solely to the unsearchable and free will of God. By definition such a miracle cannot be produced by means of an experiment: as soon as it is attacked in this manner the miracle as miracle fails to appear. A miracle remains a miracle only so long as it is unique, and it is unique even if God is not supposed to have a free will and is held to be bound by a fixed world-plan. The latter kind may fairly be called a miracle since it is unique itself and in all its phases, although some of these "phases" may be repeated from time to time, for example, in the form of a succession of inspired priests. Each priest, as he becomes inspired, remains a unique entity, who is caused to be as he is by God alone. There is here no law: it is precisely the law which destroys the miracle.

As facts are to-day a man can either believe in revelations and in inspired priests, which constitute the foundations of the Churches actually existing and of their doctrines, and in this case he remains within these communities: or else he stands without the Churches because he does not believe in their miracles. But in that case he will certainly not believe that any new miracles are genuine, and this renders it impossible that any new Church should be formed; or at any rate it becomes exceedingly improbable.

Those, therefore, who feel unable to be members of one of the historical Churches will have to make up their minds with regard to the free spirit of religion. If they wish to be full and complete men they will have to make up their minds in an affirmative sense—that is to say, they will have to acquire this spirit. This will, then, be completely their own, and they will not have the right to call themselves Christians, for example, in the strict sense, although they may approve of the ethics of Jesus, and even of the purely metaphysical part of the doctrines of the Church. (The ethics they can accept in their totality, and there will still be room for more.) In this respect men unfortunately are very lax in these days; they play with the concept of Christianity, and perhaps even go so far as to look upon it as a special form of civilization, overlooking the fact that a genuine Christianity is a dogmatic and magical Church-doctrine, which, according to the law of the excluded middle, can be accepted or not accepted, but towards which it is impossible to take up any intermediate position.

If a man has the true spirit of religion his code of ethics is given him automatically, whether he belongs to a Church or not. We may even go so far as to say that a certain specific religious disposition of his soul was the *prius*, which caused him unawares to choose one from among the various possible systems of ethics, and next to intuit explicitly one definite religion and system of metaphysics. He has thus attained enlightenment about the intellectual germs which had been lying within him, and accordingly he also sees the chosen system of ethics as being founded upon reasons: the reasons being given precisely by metaphysics and religion. His ethical intuition is perfected when he clearly apprehends its foundations, and it is just for this reason that enlightenment is of such importance practically for man from the ethical point of view.

5
DUALISM, AND HOW IT IS OVERCOME

The highest kind of enlightened intuition can give knowledge about many matters, of which the most important is the meaning of Dualism. It means that the world is composed of totality and non-totality. If it were otherwise there could be no "*it ought to be*", since there would be nothing that ought not to be. It is only when this point is reached that ethics becomes possible. If the world were a monism of order containing nothing but saints, ethics would be meaningless, and the only intuition which could exist would be a perfect intuition of totality.

We know already that man instinctively intuits in the form "it ought to be". Here dualism is presented to him in its original form. It is true that this form presents a confused picture. Thus the pursuit of ethical enlightenment necessarily is identical with the pursuit of the highest form of metaphysics; and the latter turns into religion, although this is not expressly intended.

Thus all practical ethical action has ultimately one object only—to overcome Dualism.

This end may be achieved in two ways. Reality being composed of entities, which are partly of the nature of totalities and partly of the nature of non-totalities, we may aim at the quickest and completest possible separation of these constituent parts from one another. Or else we may admit the dualism of the world, and seek to promote within it as far as possible the survival of those parts which are of the nature of a totality.

Accordingly, when a man takes up an ethical and, if he has the power, a practical moral standpoint, the fundamental nature of it will depend upon whether he resolves to adopt the first or the second means in order to overcome dualism. The resolve in turn depends upon his fundamental metaphysical convictions, and these by their nature are hypothetical—that is, a matter of conjecture.

Thus we have once more reached those considerations which were treated separately as they occurred in each one of the several sections of the book. Now that we have reached the end, we will review them once more together.

If a man believes that he can best work towards the subjection of dualism by means of his death, on the assumption that this will benefit all living beings, which in turn are supposed to be the real victims of and sufferers from dualism, then he must give up his life. Once he has made this resolve, the choice of means becomes important. Thus there are certain Indian saints who go into the wilderness in order to offer their bodies to the wild beasts for food.—Next if he believes that it is his duty to endure life, but not to do anything whatever in order to develop his powers, still less to propagate his kind, because he thinks that this conduct will tend to overcome dualism, and thus will be of service to all mankind— then he must live following the dictates of his convictions, which will cause him to practise either pure asceticism

Q

or else humble helpfulness.[1] Finally, if he believes that the development of the faculties which have been granted him is part of the world-plan, then he must follow the moral theory which has been developed in this book.

It is hardest to follow the third road consistently and without aberration, for the temptations are almost overpowering. Such temptations do not consist only in selfish impulses, but also in the permanent pressure which is exerted by the rest of the world, which has failed to reach a clear understanding of the fundamental demands of ethics. Thus, for example, that which is generally called patriotism is, as we know, no true love of neighbour or of country, or respect for the state, but is a collective-egoistic will to power, or, briefly, a sin: but those who combat this sin will reap nothing but suspicion and insult, and even, as we have seen in our days, worse.[2] Again, the man who attempts to introduce justice into social institutions will meet with nothing but opposition, at least from the "educated" classes. Here it is precisely those who have never reached a clear view about morality who oppose those who have attained such a view. The man who has reached moral vision must not allow himself to be made irresolute by such opposition, and, in fact, such opposition will not make him irresolute. He must not even allow himself to become angry or overbearing,

---

[1] Cp. Kundry's "Service" in the third act of *Parsifal*.

[2] The usual argument is, of course, that those who combat the aggressive patriotism of their own state are siding with the enemy. But if I condemn the bad manners of my side in a scientific dispute, does that imply that I am siding with the theory of my opponents?

but must be confirmed in his conviction that his path is long and thorny but is *good*, and that it is his duty to follow this path, which is the path of enlightenment, and that just because of the great resistance which he meets everywhere. For this resistance is precisely the measure of the dualism which remains to be overcome.

It is not every man who has the power to act; but every man who has had the vision has the power to teach, and that which results from the vision of the pure Teacher may confer strength to men of pure moral action whenever they act.

The demand for enlightening moral instruction in political matters is frequently countered with the objection that things will improve slowly—very slowly—of themselves. It is argued that the supra-personal entity makes use of the economic distress of all as a means of correction and that it is part of the world-plan that men are to pass to the light through darkness. Even Kant on one occasion set out these considerations in full, and they are not altogether wrong.

However, they overlook one point which has already been mentioned on several occasions, and which I repeat once more in the most general sense—a point which caused Kant in his old age considerably to modify his political Ethics.

The man who argues that things will become better of themselves overlooks that he himself, with his own particular moral vision, is a part of this automatically acting force. The argument is similar here to that of those who urge the doctrine of organic growth. They forget that the progress which is made slowly and by means of short stages does after all take place by means of *stages* and not as a continuous process, and they were unable to adduce any argument against such progress by means of *big* stages if the will to such progress, based upon right insight, existed.

The fact that I have vision, and that you have vision, is part of the world; and the same applies to mine and your will to teach, which is based upon our vision. The fact that I ought to teach what I have seen is an effective part of reality, and belongs to the category of *Realpolitik*. Further, if I experience that something is morally self-evident, the above fact is relevant to this experience in this effective manner, whether I consider myself theoretically as free or not: for in any case my consciousness allows me to look upon myself as though I were free. This fact is expressed by Luther's "I cannot otherwise".

From the point of view of practical morals the result for the man who has had vision will be a strengthening of his courage in confessing, since he will have learned that he of all men is not superfluous, that he is part of the whole, and that the supra-personal entity requires his confession. Even without this confession—provided that this thought is thinkable—things might slowly improve under the pressure of universal necessity. But, thank heaven, we need not wait for this pressure and its effects, since the confessors are at hand, as active and immediate factors in reality.

We therefore put our hope in the enlightening action of reason, since it is itself a part of reality, and because the ultimate metaphysical meaning of its existence as conscious reason seems to me to be the transcendence of dualism.

We may hope even if there is no freedom, and if we do, our hope at the same time is a faith in the reasonable rule of the ultimate foundation of the world, which makes the confessor its instrument.

On the other hand, if there is such a thing as freedom, then the confessor and man of vision can, in his own person, take a part in the formation of the Reasonable. It is true that he does not himself make the contents of his will: these are presented to him by the automatic play of his soul. But he *is* free to admit or to reject the realization of these contents—that is, their transformation into action.

Hence it would seem that there is one sole supreme commandment:

It may be said that the realization of volitional actions is controlled by motives—that is, that it is controlled in some manner, and that hence there can be no such thing as the freedom to admit or to reject. But the great problem of freedom cannot be settled in so simple a manner. When we examine the theory of suggestion, too, it looks at first as though it were wholly a matter of automatism, and as though this settled the fate of freedom once and for all. But suddenly it is perceived that, at the beginning of every process of suggestion, whether it is practised by myself or by some other person, there must stand the will or the resolution to this very process:[1] and it would appear that this is free.

The case is similar here: the logical automatism of the soul presents me with reasons for as well as against a certain action, some of which are rational, while others are merely of the nature of feelings and impulses. Now here I can resolve, once for all, to allow myself to be influenced only by reasons of a rational kind in the profoundest sense of the term. And it would appear that this resolve is free.

If, then, this is the case, then my resolve to allow myself to be influenced only by the highest and purest reason is free: if that is so, then the supreme ethical rule, which in this case would be a true rule, would run: Resolve to accept Reason.

[1] Driesch, *Grundproblem der Psychologie*, 1926, p. 217.

INDEX

Altruism, 92 *sq.*
Aristocracy, 137
Aristotle, 108, 201
Ascetics, 92, 110
Auto-suggestion, 82, 133 *sq.*,
   207

Baudouin, 229
Bees, 43
Berkeley, 181
Binet, 138
Buddhism, 219, 236

Capital punishment, 101
Categorical imperative, 22, 36,
   40, 45
China, 177
Christian Science, 179, 207
Civilization, 164 *sqq.*
Classical education, 135
Complex, 47, 132
Conscience, 96
Corporal punishment, 104 *sq.*
Coué, 132, 208, 229
Culture, 164 *sqq.*

Darwinianism, 183
Democracy, 137, 139, 185
Descartes, 195
Dichotomy, point of, 73 *sq.*,
   79, 107
Dictatorship, 141 *sq.*, 185

Entelechy, 43
Euthanasia, 101 *sqq.*

Fichte, 153, 172
Förster, F. W., 144
Freud, 208, 229

Gandhi, 180
Goethe, 32, 98
Grünbaum, 183

Hegel, 145, 147, 153, 172
Heyde, 51, 55
Holy war, 152 *sq.*, 163
Hume, 181

India, 178
Indian ethics, 65
Indian philosophy, 100
Inquisition, 152

James, William, 182
Jesus, 98, 144, 167, 238
Jung, 183 *sq.*

Kant, 16, 22 *sq.*, 29 *sq.*, 30,
   35 *sq.*, 40, 45, 62, 83 *sq.*, 91,
   144, 160, 227, 243

League of Nations, 150,
   153 *sq.*, 161, 171, 174, 187
Leibniz, 186
Lessing, Theodor, 229
Locke, 181
Lotze, 51

Magic, 32, 75 *sq.*, 90, 92, 111, 143, 237
Marriage, 119 *sq.*
Monarchy, 140 *sq.*
Money-lending, 116 *sq*
Myers, 229

Neo-platonism, 135
Nietzsche, 35, 51

Oligarchy, 140
Order, 38, 41, 45, 54
Other ego, 19

Passive resistance, 146
Patriotism, 166, 168
Phylogeny, 213 *sq.*
Pity, 34 *sq.*, 231

Quakers, 229

Realpolitik, 144
Regeneration, 43
Religions, 182
Revolution, 142
Russell, Bertrand, 144, 155

Salvation Army, 236

Scheler, 35, 42, 51, 55, 61 *sq.*, 183, 192
Schiller, 216
Schlosser, 172
Schopenhauer, 167, 170, 172
Sermon on the Mount, 65
Simeon, St., 32
Slavery, 105
Socialism, 101
Socrates, 106 ·
Spinoza, 23, 35
Spranger, 54, 183
Stoics, 135
Suggestion, 107 *sq.*, 132, 158
Suicide, 103

Tagore, 180
Teleological end, 20 *sq.*
Telepathy, 202
Tolstoy, 65, 144, 160
Treitschke, 172

Universal language, 186

Value, 51, 55 *sqq.*

Weaver bird, 43
Weber, Max, 68
Wiederhold, 51

GEORGE ALLEN & UNWIN LTD
LONDON: 40 MUSEUM STREET, W.C.1
CAPE TOWN: 73 ST. GEORGE'S STREET
SYDNEY, N.S.W.: WYNYARD SQUARE
AUCKLAND, N.Z.: 41 ALBERT STREET
TORONTO, 77 WELLINGTON STREET, WEST

A Preface to Morals
By WALTER LIPPMANN

Demy 8vo.   *Second Impression*   10s.

" There may be some other book which, if I read it, I should think a better introduction for a clear-sighted young man or woman to the actual problems of conduct in the complexity of modern civilization, but if such a book exists I have not read it."—Professor Graham Wallas in the *Nation.*

" Mr. Lippman writes admirably. His book is one of remarkable wisdom. It would be hard to find any book which treated those sexual problems which haunt the modern world more persuasively."— *Manchester Guardian.*

By the same Author:

PUBLIC OPINION.   THE POLITICAL SCENE.

The Evolution of Modern Marriage
By F. MÜLLER-LYER

Demy 8vo. Translated by I. C. WIGGLESWORTH   12s. 6d.

This is the first English translation to appear of Müller-Lyer's well-known study of man's love-relations from primitive times up to the present day. Contrary to much current pessimism on the subject, the author concludes that the new marriage in process of being evolved to-day is an ordered outcome of past and present conditions, and that in the future it may become a fuller and more beautiful relationship.

By the same Author:

THE HISTORY OF SOCIAL DEVELOPMENT

The Renewal of Culture
By LARS RINGBOM

La. Cr. 8vo. Translated by G. C. WHEELER   7s. 6d.

" Students of sociology will be very grateful to Dr. G. C. Wheeler for his excellent translation of an interesting study of social development and of the crisis confronting civilization to-day in *The Renewal of Culture* by Lars Ringbom, one of the most distinguished of modern Finnish thinkers. . . . The whole book is of real importance."— *Listener,*

Man and the Universe
By HANS DRIESCH
Demy 8vo.   TRANSLATED BY W. H. JOHNSTON   6s.

Hans Driesch is one of the ablest writers to-day on the philosophic aspects of current scientific problems. His Gifford Lectures attracted widespread attention. The present volume has been written, not for experts, but for all those interested in modern philosophic problems, and is excellently adapted to the intellectual capacities of such readers. It is inspired by a generous revolt against the domination of will and intellect, by a profound sympathy with every form of life.

The Intelligible World :
Metaphysics and Value
By PROFESSOR W. M. URBAN, PH.D.
Demy 8vo.   16s.

The general thesis of the book is that the *intelligible world*—the only world, that is, intelligible to thought—is one in which existence and value are ultimately inseparable. Reality is existence plus meaning and value. In the light of this thesis, the fundamental problems of philosophy are interpreted and a system of philosophy developed.

" A stimulating and thought-provoking piece of work. Students of philosophy can hardly fail to be impressed by the clarity of expression and the soundness of the reasoning employed."—*Church Times.*

"An important work."—*Times Literary Supplement.*

By the same Author:
VALUATION : ITS NATURE AND LAWS.

Identity and Reality
By EMILE MEYERSON
Demy 8vo.   TRANSLATED BY KATE LOEWENBERG   16s.

This is the authorized English translation of M. Emile Meyerson's well-known "Identité et Réalité" ; the author himself has written a special preface for it. The book deals with the principles of Causality, Inertia, Conservation of Energy, Time, etc., etc., and reveals a broader knowledge and a greater grasp of detail than is anywhere else to be found.